MOTHER MARY'S PATHWAY TO LOVE

*Building a loving relationship with yourself
that will transform your life*

Ohm - Mani - "Pardmay"- Umm

DANIELLE GIBBONS

Mother Mary's Pathway to Love
Danielle Gibbons

Published by Beloved Publications
Copyright © 2015 Danielle Gibbons

First Edition

Book Cover Design by BEAUTeBOOK

For all those who seek and are willing to find.

TABLE OF CONTENTS

DARK NIGHT OF THE SOUL 11

FROM OBSESSION TO REDEMPTION 27

SIMPLICITY 41

COMPLEX BY DESIGN 57

TRUST 67

I WAS UNTRUSTWORTHY 81

HEART ENERGY 87

HEART AND SOUL 101

FORGIVENESS 107

BLAME, INC. 125

ILLUSION OF SEPARATION 133

THE HARD WAY OR NO WAY 147

A SPIRITUAL LIFE 151

ON MY KNEES 165

THE SHADOW WITHIN 171

MR. HYDE 189

MIRACLES 195

JESUS ON MY TOAST 207

DOING WHAT YOU LOVE 211

SEND IN PROCRASTINATION 231

COMMITMENT 237

AN OCEAN IN A THIMBLE 253

FAITH 263

CRISIS OF FAITH 279

MOTHER MARY'S INTRODUCTION

My beloved children,

How wonderful that you have found your way to this book. I have placed within it my wisdom, my grace, and my love for each and every one of you. This book contains my experience in moving into the heart of love. It will help you to make love the center of your life, so that all that you do will come from love, will move through love, and will create more love in your life and world.

The energy I have placed within these words will move you from reading them—to experiencing them. I encourage you to use this as a workbook—*feel* your way through it— *feel* the rightness *before* you take an action. Don't do anything just because it is written. Find the truth within yourself, and *then* act. Answer the questions that I pose, take the actions that I suggest, and do the meditations that are contained within. Each step of the way, I will be with you, holding your hand, supporting you, and cheering you on. There is so much love within you and all around you. You do not have to create it, my beloved ones—you only have to awaken to its presence. I am giving you the way to do that.

I have asked Danielle to share parts of her life, and how they relate to my teachings. This way you can get a better understanding of how these teachings support your human life. The transformation that is waiting for you between the covers of this book is profound, if you will allow it. If you have found your way here, your soul is asking you not just to read this book, but to live it. Nothing will be demanded of you—nothing will even be asked of you—but if you are willing to commit to what I am offering, then I promise you will find what you need.

Thank you for your willingness to join with me on this journey. Together we can do anything. I love you.

Namaste ~

Mother Mary

DANIELLE'S INTRODUCTION

The journey to place this book in your hands encapsulates Mother Mary's teachings beautifully. It has been a labor of love for each person involved in its creation. The synchronicity Mother brought forth each step of the way has been extraordinary. Thank you for being a part of the journey.

I have served as a full body channel for Mother Mary since 1994. As you are about to discover it has been profound, and sometimes difficult, but always abundant. She came into my life unexpectedly—and from my first moment of awareness of Her, I knew I had come home. She is the foundation of my life, keeping me anchored and steady, even as She teaches me to soar among the clouds. My connection to Her is in no way exclusive. Since the beginning, I have known many who have developed an equally intimate relationship with Her. It is there for you if you seek it.

When I channel Mother, She inhabits my body in order to communicate directly with others. All twelve of Mother's teachings in this book were channeled at live events, sometimes years apart. She chose each of them, as well as the order in which they were to appear. My editor and I worked hard to stay as close to Mother's original words as possible when converting Her spoken words into written words.

In the course of my writing, I refer to Mother Mary as *Mother* with a capital *M*. The few times I refer to my birth mother, I do so using a lower case *m* to avoid confusion.

I hope that you find comfort, inspiration, and a deeper communion with yourself and the Divine within this offering. May your life be your own and your love shared with all.

Namaste ~

Danielle

CHAPTER 1
Dark night of the soul

I begin with the dark night of the soul, because it is here that you often begin your spiritual journey. If a person is happy and content with their life, they rarely seek to change it. Why would they? When a person finds themselves feeling cut off from their connection to life, love, the natural world, or divine Spirit for an extended period of time, they find themselves in the dark night of the soul, where hope and faith are rare indeed. We begin here, as so many of you already have, and then we will move into the rest of the teachings in an order that is designed to help you build a foundation for your life that can withstand anything, whether it be positive or what you perceive as negative. Of course, you can use these teachings however you wish, but I encourage you to explore and take the actions in the order they are given. You and I are about to create something extraordinary! Let's dive in.

You are given a set of signals in life which create your inner compass and give you direction, wisdom, understanding, and, ultimately, draw you toward your needed experiences. These signals are very important to understand. They are why you are doing all the self-growth and self-healing in the first place—so that you can understand what you are trying to tell to yourself. What is your soul trying to convey to you? What are your emotions trying to convey to you? What is your body trying to convey to you? What is your mind trying to convey to you?

Each one of you has a very strong signal inside of you that I would call a craving to know God. You have a very deep desire to commune with Spirit, to understand what it means to be *One*. This is a need, and a very powerful one. Some of you speak of this need, but many of you keep it private because you have grown up in a world where spirituality is confused with dogma, and individuality is not encouraged, but discouraged. No matter how often people tell you to, "be yourself, go for it, do what you want to do, be free," once they get you in a classroom it's a different story. They tell you to do it a certain way and that way only, because that is the way that it's always been done.

Because you came to this life with a slightly different agenda than the average human being (not better, not worse, just different), and your culture for the most part is not particularly supportive, this craving for spirit, for many of you, is not recognized until later in life. There may be years of not understanding this craving, and having no context in which to put it, or support in which to explore it. As a result of this, you may begin to take this craving for God and channel it into other *wants* because you do not know how to fulfill your *real* need. You find other ways to break that craving down—put a little here, a lot over there, some here, some more there—until you begin to function almost entirely from *wanting*. Because this craving for God is *so* big and runs *so* deep, you may try to fulfil it by getting your shallow *wants* met, but this will just leave you with more *wanting*! What relationship can equal the vastness of God? What item can parallel the bliss of Spirit?

Without the fulfillment of that one singular need, there begins the dark night of the soul. Some of you may be familiar with the origins of this; it was written in the context of one man's feeling of separation from God, how that made him feel, and what his experiences were. This saying—*the dark night of the soul*—pretty much encapsulates the feeling of separation from Spirit for all of you.

When you are trying to answer that craving through *want*, you create more separation and the feeling of darkness, of being alone. Even though in your spoken language, you separate feeling *lonely* from being *alone*, I would say to you that they are the same thing. When you are lonely, you feel yourself to be alone, or cut off. Even though you are meant to be in community, to take this journey together, to support one another, to uplift one another—when you feel that separation, that darkness—you begin to feel alone or lonely. When that happens, many of you seek the answer to your craving by going out and finding someone to be with. You say that you want a relationship, and ask, *"When am I going to meet my soulmate?"* Really, the answer is—simple.

When will you become one with yourself?
When will you allow that Oneness with
Spirit to dwell within you so that you do
not feel alone or lonely?

Once you do, you will no longer endlessly search for relief from your craving for wholeness in places where it does not dwell.

When you feel connected, do you notice that you don't have any *wants*? Often, you don't feel you have any *needs*, either. There is a feeling of being carried or held. When things come to you from this place, they will add positively to your life. But when they come to you from a place of separation or darkness, it does not satisfy. It may be that you are seeking to fulfill a *want* outside of yourself, rather than the *need* that is within. Your world tells you every day to seek outside of yourself—and therein is the cause of all your problems.

When people recognize the need for *Oneness* within

themselves, they will often find a place to go where they can be alone and quiet. This is why there are places in your world where people spend much of their time in silence; they recognize that the fulfillment of the need to be One with Spirit can only be found within themselves.

Some of you may have already experienced this—some of you may have experienced it a few times—but each one of you at some point will have a dark night of the soul. It is a feeling of separation that is so profound that you fear you will never find your way back. The heaviness that comes with this can be overwhelming. It's often the reason for people ending their lives. They get into the darkness and don't believe they can find their way out. I am now going to say something with the hope that you can hear it with a kind heart and an open mind. Every human being must go through this time, this dark night of the soul. Every human being is at a different point in his or her evolution, and so it may be that some people have previously obtained union with Spirit, so didn't go through it in this lifetime. You can be sure though that they went through it in their last incarnation, or one before that. I tell you this because if you do go through it in this lifetime, it's important not to get discouraged by people as you're going through it. They may say well-meaning things like, "Why are you doing this to yourself? Go take a walk, you'll feel better. Go meditate, you'll feel better. Take a pill. Do this, do that." All those things can be helpful, but the last thing that you need to hear when you are in a deep separation from God is that you are doing something wrong, or that somehow you are just not spiritual enough and you have to *do* something about it.

The dark night of the soul is necessary, because it is the final walk with deep darkness that you take as a human being. You begin your human evolution in darkness, and work your way back to the light so you can know yourself as God, and know yourself as light. When all you know is light, you cannot *see* it. You must know darkness in order to understand light. When you look out on your world and see those who are engaged in darkness—war, torture, cruelty, killing—know that they are young souls coming to explore. But as you grow away from that level of darkness, what do you replace it with? What do you do to yourself through your inability to fulfill your wants? How many years have you punished yourself? How many years have you been cruel to yourself, or cruel to someone else while trying to get what you think you want?

When you come to the lifetime of awakening, you come to the knowing that if all you had was connection with Spirit, you would be okay. If you had to, you'd give it all up— home, car, clothes, money, romance, *everything*—as long as you could keep just *one* thing—your knowledge of Spirit. When it comes to that, you make a declaration. You've come to a place in your evolution where you cannot turn back. You've passed the point of no return. As a final letting go of the darkness, you go through a dark night of the soul. Now, the man who wrote about this wasn't talking about never knowing that connection; he was talking about knowing it, feeling it, loving it, experiencing the bliss, and then losing it again—and the hell that follows.

People who are waging war and killing others are not sitting around in rooms talking about their experiences, and then coming to self-knowledge and consciousness about their acts and their deeds. They move from instinct. They don't think about it; they just do it. They jump in from a place of passion and excitement. The dark night of the soul is about understanding darkness consciously. The only way you can do that is to become conscious. When you are asleep, how do you know the essence of darkness? Darkness is the perception that you are separated from God, when you cannot be. You are never separate. When you believe that you are separate from God, you are going to act out because you think it's up to you to change things, that it all comes down to *you*. If you don't wage war, who will? You think you are on your own, that you have to figure it all out by yourself. This causes you to behave as if you are all alone and in need of protection. But when you discover the Oneness that you are, when you *feel* that Oneness, you will have to consciously let go of the darkness that still dwells within you to bring it forth. This means that every dark place within you *must* come to the light.

Sometimes it can be terrifying to face the things that are inside of you. You may not do anything outwardly that betrays your inner darkness, but it is still there inside—the rage, the desire to lash out, the want to hurt others because you are hurting. No one wants to look at these things because they are very likely the same things you put others down for. But be sure that your judgment will come back to haunt you. *Judge not lest ye be judged* is a wise thing to remember. Why? Because ultimately, *you* are always only judging *yourself*. That is what the dark night of the soul is all about—really seeing yourself— and judging what lies within. God does not judge. We don't need to either. It is something you all do to each other *and* yourselves. When you have such harsh judgments it makes it very hard to face yourself.

Spirituality is not about stepping out of
yourself and joining something out there. It
is about coming into union with what is
within. If you come to union, you must
come to acknowledgment and recognition.
For some people, depending on their level of

judgment of others and judgment of Self,
this can be the hardest thing that they will
ever do. Yet it must be done. You cannot go
around it. You can only go through it. It is
about consciously understanding exactly
what that perception of separation does to
you, and all the pain that it creates. All the
fear, all the terror, all of it; you face all of it.

Now, some of you are on the extended plan. You're experiencing the dark night of the soul a little bit at a time over a long period of time. Some of you are choosing to do it in a short period of time—one or two years. But all of you will experience a period of time in your lives when you have the connection, the communion, and feel the Oneness—and then—it's gone. And for that period of time, you cannot get it back. There's a reason for this—and it's not because you haven't figured it out, because you aren't smart enough, or spiritual enough, or because you're not meditating enough—it's because you *have* to go through it; you *must* see the darkness for what it really is. You have to look at the pain it has caused you, and ultimately, you have to see it for the illusion that it truly is. You have to see it for the human construct that it is. You have to understand how it works within your life, and within you.

There are all kinds of things that can bring on a dark night of the soul. Often it arrives after a great loss. You'll hear people on television or in print say that they were, "very religious and devout, and had great faith", but then this *thing* happened to their child, or bank account, or job... and now they don't want anything to do with God. God has forsaken them.

Christ had his dark night of the soul upon the cross. *God, why hast thou forsaken me?* is a powerful perception. I want to speak of this because all of you are in different places in your growth, in your evolution, and when you come to this time, please don't blame yourselves. Always, I endeavor to help you understand the deeper aspects of spirituality. Yes, I can help you manifest things externally, and that's fine; I am happy to serve in that capacity. But more than anything, I want you to be at peace within yourself. In order to do that, you must be conscious. Part of the journey of consciousness is facing the demons within, the demons that tell you to go to sleep, to answer your craving for God with food, or money, or a new piece of jewelry, or a car, or a new love, or a dog, or whatever will fill the longing temporarily. The demons within push you to eat that food, or buy that car, and are then quite happy to inform you that it's not enough and that you need more and more and more and more and more and more and more. That is the darkness. That is the separation.

> When you are connected, you don't feel
> those wants. They are gone.

Be careful of what your mind says to you about what I'm telling you—the darkness within you that thrives off your separation from God will tell you, "Oh, no! No way! *I'm* not going to go through the dark night of the soul! " Or it will tell you that *this* isn't the brand of spirituality that you want—you just want the good stuff—you want it to be all about happiness and never about anything else. Or, alternatively, you can open yourself to the feeling and know that it is part of your evolution to Oneness, so when it comes, you won't punish yourself for having it. You will be kind to yourself. You will stand up for yourself if people say that maybe you're not doing enough.

To sit with the dark night of the soul
because you love yourself enough to accept
every part of yourself, every aspect of your
being—to know that nothing inside of you
is so dark that you cannot forgive it, and
then, to love it, accept it, and then finally to
let it go, takes *willingness*.

For each of you, I can tell you that the dark night of the soul plays on your most prominent issues. If it's a feeling that life is not fair and you have self-pity, there will be a time when you feel as though you're drowning in it. Sometimes sickness can accompany this, or a feeling of exhaustion and fatigue, because during the dark night of the soul, there is a part of you that *is* dying; the part that believes you are separate, alone, and without help; the part that thinks that no one really loves you or cares about you deeply. It is your *illusions* that are dying. After watching millions upon millions of people go through this over and over and over again, I have seen that human's false beliefs rarely have graceful deaths. They tend to be loud and messy with lots of, "Why *me*? Why *this*?" And pain. There will be pain. For some people, the dark night will bring about suicidal thoughts for the first time, and they may begin to plan their deaths. Sometimes a deep depression sets in and creates emotional paralysis, or the inability to hold down a job, or function in the greater world. Sometimes years of pent-up rage comes out, in shocking or surprising ways.

Whatever is dark within you, will eventually come to light. The reason that I brought up *craving* to begin this conversation, was to assist you in recognizing your signals.

When you are craving something other
than God—stop, look, and listen. Listen
closely to what is going on inside of you.

This is going to be a little tricky, because you have all had years of channeling these other cravings into all kinds of subcategories. You don't pay attention to them, because some of you have become very clever and haven't put all the craving eggs in one basket, so you're not drunk, or obese, or on heroin, or having sex with all kinds of people all the time. What you have done, though, is to put the cravings into little, small things, those things that you just do every day, every day, throughout the day. You don't notice that you are trying to feed something that cannot be sated. Think about some of the categories of things that are not particularly healthy for you. I'll give you some of my favorite categories.

One is the craving to be entertained. Now, this is different than the need to experience a performance. The want to be entertained is you wanting to shut down and you want something or someone else to fill that gap. You're going to go to sleep and set your alarm clock, and then you want everyone else to feed you. This is why your television, and often your films, are toxic for the mind, the body, and the emotions. They are designed for you to switch off. You go to see a big movie where lots of explosions occur and you pretty much have the plot within the first 5 minutes. The rest of the time you can just switch off.

Think about that—the want to be entertained versus the need to experience a performance. When you are experiencing a performance, you are energetically and emotionally involved. Even if you are not in the presence of a live performance, it becomes a co-creation. If you are spending time watching things that you are not co-creating with, turn it off and ask yourself:

What do I really need right now?
What do I really need?

One of my other favorite categories is sugar. Refined sugar has no place in the body. It does nothing to the body except punish it. It is designed chemically like other gateway drugs are designed—to make you want more. Literally, that is how it works in the body. It pushes a lot of energy through and then leaves you with none, even as the body says that it needs more. You need more, you need more, and you need more. The body is trying to tell you it needs more energy, not more sugar, but if this is one of your subcategories for craving, then you will interpret the signal as needing more sugar. Even if you are not eating a cake a night, watch how you weave it into your days and your weeks. A little bit here, a little bit there, a bit here, a bit more there.

Again, watch how you have put all your little cravings into categories. When you are craving sugar, when you *want* sugar, nothing, I can promise you, beloved ones, nothing in your beautiful, healthy bodies ever says, "Oh, I need a cookie for nutrition right now. This body needs a cookie because only in the depths of that chocolate chip does the salvation of my cells live." When you pick up that refined sugar, you are picking up a *want*. Again, that *want* in you tells you it's never enough, so you have to have more tomorrow, please. Or, you may have to have more *right now*.

Refined sugar helps to turn your physical body off. Over time, it actually has a dulling effect on your whole body, so that when the physical body is trying to tell you something, it's very difficult for you to understand; the sugar starves those cells of what they need and blocks the ability of the nerves to communicate with you. It throws many of the body's systems out of balance, one at a time, so that when your body tries to tell you something, the message cannot get through. Ultimately, this will put you in a place of numbness and wanting more.

Next is any activity that looks very good at the outset, but at a certain point as you are engaged in it, starts to feel heavy, or maybe makes you a little headachy; that is a signal that you are using it as a means of escape. It may be a hobby like reading, or something else that you really enjoy doing, but understand that when you do too much of it, you are using it as a means of escape. The more sensitive you become, the more you will be able to discern when you pass over from enjoyment to escapism. When you start to feel that discomfort, that heaviness, though just the hour before you were enjoying yourself, and you keep going anyway, even as it gets worse, ***STOP!***

> Put down what you are doing and ask
> yourself,
> *"What do I need?*
> *What am I really craving?*
> *How do I need to connect with The One right*
> *now?"*

The last category I will speak about is spending too much time with one person or group of people, and it doesn't matter whether they are coworkers, children, parents, or friends; when you begin to feel that same heaviness you feel when you over-do an activity, that is your sign that you are using them to fill an emptiness within yourself that you don't want to face and fulfill on your own. You can allow people to support you, but when you try to use them to fill yourself up you overstep the boundary of their support. All of a sudden they begin to irritate you. You don't want to be around them, but you continue being around them anyway. You keep staying. Again, that is a signal that you are trying to use others to fulfill something within yourself. You've all felt these things. I'm making this very simple—you've all felt the things I describe in each of these categories.

Regardless of how much you want to rebel from it, you *are* on a spiritual path. The more you are willing to acknowledge this, the more you will fulfill the original craving for Spirit and ultimately get you what you really want, which is Oneness. This doesn't mean that you'll never eat a cookie again or go to a movie where things blow up and all of that. It might mean that, but it doesn't have to. It will be what it is for each one of you, unique unto you.

The last thing that I will mention in relation to the dark night of the soul is that there may well up within you a rage towards God that is old, old, old. All your feelings about what you've perceived God has not done in your life and the lives of others—the disappointments that you've carried for lifetimes—this is when it comes to a head; because ultimately, that darkness is the rejection of God, of being separate, of feeling yourself apart from and rejecting God, rejecting Spirit. Ultimately, once you've rejected God, you have to reject yourself. It is hard to work through.

When you find yourself in your dark night
of the soul, what you must do is find
support. Do not—do *not* try to go through it
alone. I am planting these words within
your soul, in your heart, so that whatever
lifetime you come to it in, you will
remember my words. Find support. Maybe

you have to educate the people that you
want support from and tell them, "Don't fix
me. Don't tell me to go take a walk. If I get
to be too much, let me know, and let me *be*.
Help me, and when I get through this I'll
turn around and do the same for you." Look
to the categories I have just discussed and
pause before you react and reach for the old
cravings. Remember your true craving is
for God, and abstain from those things that
feed the darkness and separation as best
you can, and trust it will be enough.

If you've already had your dark night, please, when you meet someone who is having his or hers, check your impatience and remember—you don't know how long it's going to take him or her to wake up. You didn't know how long it was going to take you, so don't lose your patience for yourself or others. This doesn't mean that you have to be at their beck and call. When you go through the dark night of the soul, you can be a little crazy, very dark, very negative, and not the life of the party. But you all go through it. All of you are moving to Oneness, it is the community in which you exist. You must acknowledge and accept that you are a part of it and that it is a part of you. Do what you can for that community so that that community can be there for you.

It takes great courage to face yourself, and in the facing, to love yourself, to not punish yourself for what you find, but instead, to accept and surrender what is there. And then, and then, that craving for Oneness, that need to be one with Spirit, is fulfilled. Forever. You never go back. You never forget.

MEDITATION:

Sit on a cushion on the floor, or in a chair with your feet flat. Close your eyes, and as you breathe, imagine you are looking at yourself. See and feel a living, breathing image of yourself.

As you face yourself, say a prayer that you are willing to see, to know, and to love all that is within you.

As you face yourself, connect with the knowing that darkness is simply a different aspect of the light, and that you simply desire to move beyond that darkness. Commit to knowing that love will flow through it all, even as you endure your dark night of the soul. Breathe in the image of yourself, and see the love that surrounds you. As you continue to breathe in your loving image, let it be absorbed throughout your whole body. Do not fear what you cannot control. Focus instead on the choices that you make each day. Know what you can control, and whether you are feeling in darkness or in light—you make your own choices, always.

And always choose love, choose love, choose love.

Take three deep breaths and gently let go of the meditation.

I thank you for allowing me to serve you. It has been a great joy.

Namaste ~

CHAPTER 2
From obsession to redemption

I feel it is imperative to let you know I am not a candidate for sainthood. I believe Mother chose me to channel Her because I was such a crazy mess. I am the ambassador for the *If I can do it, anyone can* brand of growth through spirituality. Let me explain. When I first surrendered to a spiritual way of life, I was lost within an addiction to food that had me bound tightly to insanity. I was saturated in self-pity and almost every motivation that emerged from inside of me was centered on getting what I wanted. I had lost hope that I could have a good life, and so set a course for destruction. I didn't start out that way, but that's where I ended up before Mother burst into my consciousness like water to my parched soul.

She asked me to write about our journey together in relation to each of the teachings. These teachings, like all Mother's teachings, have had a profound and life altering effect on me. They have impacted my daily perceptions at the deepest possible levels of my psyche. I have changed, of course, but not into someone else. I have just become more myself. Let me go back a bit and show you.

I was startled when Mother chose to begin this book with *The Dark Night of the Soul*. It felt stark and unsettling. I felt that if I wrote about this it would be too much like letting you look down my pants, just having met. But as soon as I read it, I thought, *yes, of course, this is where it always begins—at least for me anyway*.

Kahlil Gibran described my odyssey with food precisely when he wrote:

The lust for comfort, that stealthy thing that enters the house a guest, then becomes a host, and then the master.

My earliest memories are centered around sugar. Whatever form it came in on birthdays and holidays, it brought me excitement and comfort. It was always there for me. Sugar captured my desire at five, and held me hostage for twenty-three years.

At eighteen, I crossed the line from craving to addiction. My dark night began when my addiction had progressed to the point where I couldn't stop binging. Food was the first thing I thought of when I woke in the morning and the last thing I mourned before I went to sleep at night. Food and body image took up every available thought throughout my day. I became its slave and it my master. My addiction held me underwater until I was willing to grow gills.

A happy, optimistic child by nature, I loved life. I spent most of my time playing outside with a big group of neighborhood friends. Barefoot, skinned knees, and tangled hair, I moved with athletic grace and enthusiasm whether our games took place in water, at the community pool, or the grassy fields and lawns that comprised my neighborhood. I spent hours lying on the Earth feeling connected to the world around me. That connection gave me a strong sense of self. I wasn't aware of this consciously until I lost my connection to nature and myself, which I did, one binge at a time.

We moved every few years and finally settled in Birmingham Alabama, the buckle on the Bible belt. The good people of the south loved college football and Jesus, in that order, but what they did best was smile and say everything is fine when the house was burning down around them—a valuable skill I was soon to need.

Our modest ranch home proclaimed our middle class

life. My father, a tall charismatic alcoholic, spent most of his time parked in his faux leather lounger, yellowed by nicotine, with the television on, a cigarette in one hand, and a glass of scotch in the other. My mother, a long legged beauty with green eyes and chestnut colored hair, was a former can-can dancer from Germany who moved to the United States from post-war Berlin looking for opportunity. I know she loved me deeply, but I often felt her desire to be somewhere else, away from the burden of responsibility that seemed to rest primarily on her shoulders. Our best times were spent cuddling. It was my mother's way of showing me that safe havens exist, even if they are not always obvious.

By the seventh move in ten years, she'd had enough and divorced my father. She married her dentist boss and found her security. A few months after their wedding, my grandmother died from old age. She had given me the best summers of my life on Kelly's Island in Lake Erie. Three months later my dog died. She was the keeper of my heart. My father, who had been battling lung cancer for over a year, died three months after that. I was thirteen.

The world was indeed flat and I'd just fallen off the edge. I somehow managed to keep a smile on my face, and place one foot in front of the other. I told anyone who asked that I was just fine. But I was full of holes that I didn't even know were there, so possessed no ability to fill them in a loving way. I turned to the one thing I knew would sooth— *sugar*. I imagined myself living in my favorite board game, Candy Land. I slid down the peppermint slide and jumped into the chocolate lake with both feet. I ate as much sugar as I could get my hands on.

After a year or so, I began to feel like a forest animal constantly alert to danger. I felt as though I were strung too tight, as though I were wearing my skin inside out. Overly sensitive, I easily became overwhelmed by life. I needed the sugar coating between the rest of the world and me.

Throughout my childhood my body was as skinny as a starlet just out of rehab. I didn't start gaining weight until the age of eighteen, so no one suspected my craving was waging a campaign, executed with military precision, to take over my life. They just thought I had a sweet tooth.

My first memory of insanity came when I was seven years old. I would sit on the faded linoleum kitchen floor, gazing into the depths of the lazy-susan cabinet, spinning the top shelf and hoping it would contain something sweet (even though I knew it didn't). I watched a small orange box of unsweetened baking chocolate spin past my eyes; once, twice, three times, until it called out for me to stop. I knew how it would taste, yet I also knew I would eat it. I went back to it over and over again, and ate at least one small square of that chocolate each time, hoping it would be transformed into something sweet.

I lost complete control of my eating when I was seventeen. Soon after, I lost control of my life. Sugar became like air for me. My therapist in New York once suggested I give it up after I alluded to possibly eating too much and I burst into tears, startling us both. Neither of us ever brought it up again.

Performing on stage in high school productions quieted my fear of life. I was in the moment, fully myself, while pretending to be someone else. *Bliss.* I decided to become an actress, but the play always ended and the curtain always came down. I used drugs, alcohol, and cigarettes to numb the pain between acts.

At sixteen, I wanted to look sexy, but usually ended Saturday nights with my head in the toilet after drinking too much beer and cheap wine. The drugs helped fill the emptiness inside with laughter, and outrageous theories about how the world would be, if only my friends and I were in charge.

Taking a copious number of diet pills was my first diet plan, with the added bonus of letting me get a lot done without being present in my body. I felt I needed the attention of boys to validate my worth, and believed that if I became the fat friend I would cease to exist. Period.

A friend taught me to binge when I was seventeen. It was my first love affair with food. Since I had a job, I could finance it all on my own. I spent hours gathering all the perfect binge foods. I was even willing to go to multiple stores to get just the right bags of chips, cookies, chocolate bars, or the frozen desserts I never waited to thaw before eating. I loved the sweet, salty, crunchy taste on my tongue. I ate it all down to the crumbs and licked the oily salt off every finger until my heart and body hurt.

It was a relief to feel full. Every binge inserted itself between me and myself. At nineteen, I crossed the line from heavy use of food to cope with my life, into addiction. There was no going back. Hearing my inner voice was like trying to hold water in my hands.

After a disappointing year at college in Boston, I moved to New York seeking fame when I was twenty years old. The energy of the city galvanized me and I seriously began to pursue my acting career. It seemed to me that all the beautiful people of the world must live in Manhattan. The Sikh cab drivers with their regal turbans looked like pasha's who had traded their thrones for a cab, honking and shouting at me to get out of the way; the smell of borscht, lo mein, and the best pizza outside of Italy, mixed with the excrement on the streets and made being a pedestrian an experience that engaged all the senses. I haunted the museums. Seeing the original creations rather than a print changed my relationship to art. When I found something I loved, my whole body vibrated with excitement and a smile spread over my face. I could feel the energy of the piece and for the first time, understood completely why someone would pay so much to have it in their home.

One evening while I was riding the subway, a man brandishing a battered saxophone held our train car hostage. He told us he would play until everyone gave him some money. He made the most awful screeching and wailing sounds with it. I thought my eardrums were going to desert me, never to return. Needless to say, he left with bulging pockets and we were left with admiration after being subjected to the best gorilla marketing campaign we had ever encountered. All of it made me want to belong to this glorious mish-mash of a place. But my insidious addiction constantly whispered poison in my ear: *All this is for them, never for you.*

After two years of failed attempts at jumpstarting my acting career, my binges had escalated to daily events. I was afraid to continue forging a career that left me open to constant rejection. My inner compass was gone, and it left me feeling as if I were homeless. With every food binge, line of cocaine, and drink of alcohol, I betrayed myself. I began to suspect that if I did manage to become a successful actress, my appetites would kill me. I made sure I was too hungover from either sugar, alcohol, cocaine, or some combination, to make any open auditions for acting jobs. I was the saboteur of my dreams. My dark night had begun.

I finally got my own apartment. There were now no roommates or family to hide my binges from. Weariness had settled into my soul and food had ceased to be a comfort, but had instead become the tormentor. For the first time in my life, I found cynicism and sarcasm preferable to the honest joy of living. I no longer held the same love of life I had as a child. I felt disconnected, as if I were watching my life, rather than living in it. I could still have fun and laugh with friends, but often felt like I was faking it.

I began to worry that something was wrong with my eating when I gained twenty-five pounds in a few months, despite restricting my meals, taking high impact, one-and-a half hour long aerobics classes every day, and using cocaine two or three nights a week. It seemed obvious to me that if I was eating too much, I should take a break from eating all together and adopt the starvation diet plan; drinking only liquids for two weeks at a time, or until all the weight came off.

The battle raged for two years. I binged and starved my way through gaining and losing the same forty pounds every four to six months. Every time I lost the weight, I was a good girl. When I gained it back, I was a bad girl, and the cruel voice inside me became merciless in its criticism of me. My addiction scooped out my bright and shiny Self and left me hollow.

The addict's motto should be, "Run first and ask questions never." At a friend's urging, I moved to Los Angeles. On the outside I displayed my disdain for la-la-land and its blonde glory with pride, but inside I felt desperate for something, anything to happen. Living with a roommate helped stem the tide of my addiction for a short while, until I figured out how to conceal my habit. Keeping track of his nightly schedule (as if I were his personal secretary) left me free to binge without the threat of discovery.

Adrenalin pumped through my body as I pulled up outside my apartment, grocery bags filled with my crunchy, salty, sweet fixes. I would hurry into my room and shut the door. Alone, I arranged myself on the bed so that if anyone walked into the room unexpectedly, my bag of food would be hidden between my body and the wall. I would lose myself in a fantasy novel so I wouldn't feel the shame of eating like a feral creature. I didn't even taste what I was eating anymore, and chewed just enough to get it down my throat.

Like a credit card, my bill had come due. In the same way tree roots tear apart sidewalks when they have grown too big to be contained, my emotions had begun punching through the barrier made of food I had placed between my awareness and what was really going on inside me. I began experiencing intense bouts of rage that dissolved into bitter tears of self-pity. I felt as though I was drowning in dark feelings of blame, and I wanted to lash out and hurt others because I was hurting.

At that time I lived a block from Venice Beach. I ran on the beach any morning I wasn't hungover, and at first there weren't many. One morning I saw a small pod of dolphins swimming not far from shore, past a section of beach where I had stopped to catch my breath. As their sleek backs broke the surface of the water, joy surged up inside me, silencing the chaos in my head for the rest of the day. I saw the dolphins every few weeks after that, and slowly things began to change. Their presence had allowed space to grow inside allowing me to breathe.

Around the same time as the dolphins, my friend Cassy showed up on my doorstep at 2 am, begging me to help her with her cocaine problem. When I met her two years before, she had been a vibrant, whimsical young woman. Chestnut hair and eyes that twinkled with mischief, she charmed everyone she met. What now stood on the threshold of my apartment was a gaunt, hollow-eyed ghost of the woman I knew. Her light was doused, and in her eyes a paranoid darting had replaced the twinkle.

She told me her obsession with cocaine had gotten so bad that she couldn't shower anymore, because she was paranoid someone would break through her securely locked apartment door, *and* the locked bathroom door, and steal her stash. She would poke her head out from behind the shower curtain every few seconds while showering to make sure it was by the sink where she left it. I stared at her in shock. I knew she was using daily, but had no idea what a hold it had on her until that moment. I had never thought to discourage her, because until only a few months before, I was partying right alongside her. My use was never as frequent, or as much, but who was I to cast the first stone? I had gotten fed up with feeling so ragged from cocaine and heavy drinking that I was able to stop, because I never obsessed over drugs and alcohol the way I did with food.

The next morning, I called a group of people who specialized in helping others recover from cocaine addiction. Over the next few weeks, they helped her find a way back into her life. The first three months I went to meetings to celebrate her sobriety milestones. I heard a common theme emerging from the stories of obsession with drugs and alcohol. Like my friend's shower story, everyone had their own rituals around using that were perceived as vital to their survival. As I listened to these people, it echoed my relationship with food.

I admitted to Cassy that I had a problem with sugar. I was inspired by her sobriety so I swore to give up sugar for good. I lasted three weeks, but lied and said I was still abstaining six weeks later when I wasn't.

One night, I was digging in the garbage to retrieve half my binge only an hour after I had thrown it away, vowing never to binge again. My body felt out of my control while my mind was screaming at me to stop. Fueled by obsession and filled with shame, I dug past the old banana peel, used tissues, and egg shells tacky with hardened whites, hair, and God knows what else I had thrown on top earlier to hide the plastic bag I had stuffed my snacks in. I opened the bag and pulled out the Pepperidge Farm Geneva cookies and half of a large bag of Fritos and finished off every crumb.

My bottom came rushing up to meet me. I was full to bursting. I could only take small sips of air because my stomach took up all the room inside me. My heart was pounding from too much sugar and my palms were sweating. I felt as though I needed to run screaming outside or vomit for days as a suffocating darkness closed over my head. It swallowed me whole and I knew it would never let me back up into the light and air. I panicked. *Something* pulled me off the couch and propelled me down the hall to Cassy's apartment, lifted my arm to knock on the door, and made me wait long enough to have it open.

I lurched into her apartment with tears streaming down my face, and told her what I had just done and that I had been lying for weeks. The relief I felt by telling her the truth opened up a space inside me to breath, just like the dolphins had. I knew sharing this was the right thing for me. The next morning she helped me find a group that specialized in food addiction. After all, we were in Los Angeles where you couldn't throw a rock without hitting a recovering addict.

I don't remember much about that first gathering we went to, except that those people were just like me and I belonged among them. The good people there told me I had a disease. Like cancer or AIDS, there was no cure, only a daily sense of wellness based on my willingness to substitute all my old behaviors with food for new behaviors based on spiritual principals. I really had no idea what these people were talking about, but they were nice and seemed sincere in their own miraculous restoration to health. I attended different gatherings a few days a week and began to experience hope that I could get beyond this crippling disease, and in equal measure, dread about what I would have to give up.

Unlike some addictions, I couldn't abstain from food all together. But I could abstain from the foods that triggered a binge. Sugar was the worst offender; snack foods were a close second. A more experienced woman from the group told me I could get well by abstaining, and working through my issues using their structure with the help of God and the rest of the group. I actually thought that I didn't have any issues, except where food was concerned. I believed if I could just figure out the right way to eat that everything would be fine.

I felt determined to do as she suggested, but the only God I knew was sugar. The thought of giving it up even for a day left me anxious and trying to justify why I needed just *one more binge*. I arrived late to every meeting and I left early so no one would talk to me. I never shared. I binged after each one and would swear to start over on Monday. But Monday came and went and I found another excuse to put it off. It was baffling. I couldn't stop overeating even though I desperately wanted to, and even though I had been given the tools and the structure I needed to do it. I felt some relief when I was able to abstain from sugar for a few months, but I wasn't taking enough action to bring about the change I needed in order to pull myself out of the hole I was in.

After seven months I had stopped communicating with the woman who was helping me, and dropped all the meetings I'd been attending except one, which was a women only group that met on Monday nights. By now I was binging even worse than before. I weighed one-hundred and twenty pounds and stood five feet, seven inches tall. I was twenty-seven years old and could barely hold down a job. I was always late on my rent. I spent hours at the gym every day. I had just lost thirty pounds by starving myself again, and felt ancient. Almost every thought in my head centered on food or my body.

One Monday night as I sat in the women's group listening to a young woman share her story with food addiction, I decided this wasn't working for me. I made the decision to stop going all together. Immediately a deep, sonorous, *male* voice spoke to me from outside my mind, as if he were sitting in the metal folding chair next to me. In a firm voice laced with kindness, I heard him say, *"If you do not work this program, you will die"*

The resonance of truth rushed through my body like dammed water released by a flood. In a flash I could feel the steady crush of my Spirit with every cruelty I had inflicted on myself. In that moment I experienced the divide within, and knew I would do anything to get across it and back to myself.

I whipped around in my chair and asked the woman behind me if I could speak to her. I admired her after hearing her tell her story the week before, and hoped she would help me. She nodded yes. I spent the next hour fidgeting in my seat, waiting for the meeting to end. After it was over, I practically leapt on her in my need to get started. I had not been so far gone that I would ignore a literal come to Jesus moment. I asked her if she would help guide me in getting well. She agreed but told me she had a strict structure I had to follow if I wanted to work with her. In that moment I would have crawled over hot coals to have the kind of serenity I saw in her, so my answer—*yes*—came easily.

As I began to follow her guidance, I stopped binging and starving. After a few months, a curious thing started to happen; I began to wake up happy for no reason. She warned me that I would be unable to keep this feeling unless I embraced a version of God that supported my growth. I hated that in the beginning, because I didn't *want* God to be the answer. Powerlessness never sat well with me. *I* wanted to be the answer. She suggested I start getting on my knees to pray, even though I didn't yet have a relationship with God; I didn't even know what I wanted God to be. She asked:

> Why don't you let God show up in the way
> you need it to be?

Great, I thought, feeling confident nothing would show up at all. It was so easy to ignore the fact that a disembodied voice had already spoken to me! I promised her that I'd do as she asked. So, cursing her and feeling ridiculous, one morning I got out of bed, went down on my knees, and spoke aloud a prayer of surrender. Immediately, I was filled with a force so extraordinary that I wept. A feeling of beauty revived me, and I felt wrapped in the safety of my mother's arms, just as I had as a little girl before loss and addiction snatched me from them. I was in the presence of an angel. Her light felt sustaining, like a new form of nourishment. She spoke in my heart, *"I am the one who comes before."* I didn't understand what she meant, but I knew I was safe. I was home.

This heralded the end of the dark night of my soul. I had no idea how far from the Spirit of life I had gone until I was reunited with it. I realized that those two years were about marinating in my darkness, so that I would be willing to live a life of service and devotion. I know myself well enough to realize that the voice spoke the truth. I would have taken my own life if I had continued to live, day after day, feeling separated from myself. I didn't have a partner, children, or a career I was passionate about to anchor me to this world. I had been existing, but not *living*. To feel disconnected was, and still is, the worst way I can imagine to live.

Not a day goes by that I don't feel grateful for the gift of reconnection to people, the divine, and the life that pulses all around and within me. I know that Mother Mary in Her infinite wisdom brought me to the brink, held me there long enough to experience separation, and then brought me back to life. I have earned my gills.

CHAPTER 3
Simplicity

It is vital that you keep things simple because it is from this energy that all things flow with greater grace and ease in your life. It is from here we begin to build your foundation. As you grow in your spiritual life, you make important, conscious decisions to create changes that you feel you have needed and wanted for a long time. You are choosing your own fulfillment. You are choosing life. You are choosing love. You are choosing peace.

In your culture, these are often not the popular choices. Simplicity is not easy. It goes against certain belief structures that are put into place to maintain the element of darkness, not only in your individual life, but also in your collective life. Things work out a bit better for each of you when you choose the simpler route over the more complicated one—so, why is it so often a struggle to choose the simple way over the complicated way?

Your culture shares broad beliefs about simplicity. The number one belief you all hold collectively about simplicity is that it is boring—that somehow, if you choose the simple way, your life will also become boring, and not much will happen—nothing interesting or noteworthy, anyway, and certainly nothing on a big or grand scale. Whether you consciously desire it or not, that which is engrained in the collective tells you that if you are not living a big, glamorous life, then somehow you are not living the way you ought to.

This is not only about American culture. Think about food for a moment. How long do you think most restaurants would stay in business if they sold just the same simple fare from one day to the next to the next? In some cultures, that's okay, but in most it is not, because there is something inside of you that you call drive, or ambition.

Many of you are learning, or relearning, how to channel this in a way that is healthier and more kind. You do not have to give up things that you feel drawn to just because they are big and require numerous steps to complete.

> You are coming to understand that it is the way you go about finding fulfillment that matters.

There is a drive or ambition, collectively, to be the best. Whether it's the best country, the best sports team, or the best whatever it may be—food, good looks, a big house or fancy clothing—as long as you are the best, collectively or individually, then you've reached your goal or made it to the finish line.

Your country is experiencing a very poignant decline in your place as number one in the world. You can see this by how your government is scrambling to try to regain its position as number one. You often hear in the news and in the way people talk that it is about repairing the damage, coming back to being number one, and taking your rightful place at the head of the line. This is a pervasive idea in the collective consciousness, and very intense in the United States.

For those of you who are trying to do things differently, it will be hard to break away and go against the stream because there is the collective flow, and then there is the flow that is underneath. The flow that is underneath is the flow of Spirit, the flow of God. It's often easy to get caught up in the upper flow of your culture and outside world, and when you do you'll frequently have a hard time finding the flow running underneath.

If you slip off a rock and fall into the river, it is going to carry you. Sometimes you step into the flow of the river and it takes a while before you can grab a branch and slow yourself down enough to say:

> *Wait*—is this the river that I *want* to be in? Is this the flow I want carrying me at this point in my life? There are two main elements to simplicity that go against the flow of your society; one is slow, the other is quiet. To choose the life of simplicity, to choose that energy, it will always ask you to slow down and to get quiet. If you go on the premise that these are the two main ingredients in simplicity, and if you think in terms of applying this premise to everything in your life—how you walk, how you breathe, how you drink, how you eat, how you prepare your food, how you prepare your body, how you step out into the world, how you drive your car, how you ride the train, how you travel, how you interact with others, how you go about your profession, how you work with money, how you apply that to your spirituality—and think in terms of slow and quiet, then you will make things easier for yourself.

These things often sound great on paper, but how do

you actually apply them to the situations that come up in your life, like when you're running late, when you haven't prepared for something you are suddenly asked to do, when you're hungry, or you've forgot something and have to run around to handle it, or when someone is having an emergency and they're asking you to help or to participate?

All of a sudden you are faced with a choice—either slipping off that rock, taking action, and jumping into the rushing river of the larger collective, where you're not sure when a branch will present itself, so you can slow yourself down and regroup, or you can choose the quieter river that flows underneath, where you are floating and free to get in and out any time that you wish, or to stop all together.

For the next week, let slow and quiet be your mantra all day, every day.

See where it applies, where you are challenged, and how much fear it brings up. Fast and loud in the collective flow is exciting and very glamorous, with a lot going on, many ingredients, and a lot of color and brightness. And that may be fun at times, but you must understand that energetically, *fast and loud drowns out the still, small voice.*

I like that it's called the still, small voice, because it evokes an image of something inside of you that is infinitely peaceful and doesn't need to shout and jump around to get your attention. It doesn't need to pull you in and say, *"You're going to listen to me now!"* It just abides quietly within you. It's in that place where you come face to face with the knowledge that *you have the power to choose.*

You are empowered from birth with free will, with choice. It's inside of you, waiting. Your fast, loud Self must come to it. It's not going to come and grab you in the middle of noise and confusion. It's not going to shout to be heard.

What your still, small voice *will* do is hold your hand to let you know it's there. But if you're too loud and too fast, you won't notice that something is holding your hand, or that there is something infinitely peaceful abiding within you.

The rest of the world, at this point in time, is not thriving on simplicity. It craves chaos, the fast and loud, because it cannot hear that still, small voice. The problem is, however, that once you're loud and fast, you have to keep being louder and faster to be heard, to be seen, and to be acknowledged in a society that is becoming faster and faster and louder and louder by the minute.

Individuals who choose the life of simplicity must decide that they don't need to be heard anymore, and are ready to step out of the cacophony and just go slowly, be quiet, and figure out what is exciting for *them*.

Simplicity is never boring.
That is the excuse that people use to justify
the loud and the fast.

Boredom comes in those moments when loud and fast just isn't quite loud and fast enough. When there is a space between events, some people just want to fill it as fast as they can, because inevitably, simplicity forces you back to yourself, to your still, small voice. It leads you to face the things about yourself that you've been talking over, making noise to cover, or running very fast away from. Given your own struggles with these things, it's no wonder that it's not the popular movement on your planet.

Looking at the darkness or the gray within is rarely a happy experience. At best, you feel the rightness of that exploration and absolutely know that for yourself, this is the path you've chosen for your life.

Knowing that you have chosen this path of consciousness, also know that the only way to thrive on this path is through a simple life.

There are some interesting things to think about and to meditate on. No matter what you are engaging with out in life, find the simplicity within the complexity. For example, look at the human body; if you were to study every little bit of it, it would be a lot of information and seemingly very complex.

In actuality, the way that every single thing in the body articulates and works together to create one human being is really quite simple. One pathway leads to the next to the next to the next to the next. The interconnectedness is very simple in its overall design, but appears complex because there is so much in its design.

Don't be fooled by things that are presented to you in a very complex way, whether it concerns relationships, career choices, changes in your meditation practice, eating—or whatever—don't be fooled by complexity. Do not allow your mind to trick you into turning something very simple into something very complex so that you can sabotage yourself.

Scientists and engineers in your culture look at seemingly complex issues and find them interesting. They want to study them. They like to take things apart, see how everything works, and then maybe see if it can go back together again in the same or a different, new way. But it is a small percentage of the population that thinks this way.

For most of you, when something begins to get too complex, your mind shuts off and you don't want to pursue it. It's too hard. It's too much. So you either stop doing what you're doing or you go in a different direction. Be careful that you do not allow the mind to take simple concepts and make them complex so that you'll give up on them. For example, I recently recommended to some who had attended a workshop that they try slowly and gently, over time, increase their breathing capacity. *Breath*—a simple idea. You understand it and the basic need for it, and a little bit of what it does for your body.

What some of you do is take a simple suggestion to take a simple action and make it very complex. You begin to think that you have to set aside time, go to a breathing coach, and then you make the excuses of no money or time, no space, and now all of a sudden an energy of complexity is introduced into a very simple concept. It then becomes very easy to justify not doing that very simple something.

Collectively, you are all trained to make things complicated. There is a belief that complicated equals important. If something is very complicated, then people are doing very important things. There are some people who take these simple things and deliberately make them complicated so that you will not want to be a part of it or try to discover what is really there for you—then they can serve as the authority on that particular something. But most things, when broken down to their basic elements, are fairly simple.

As you move into changes and new endeavors, look at slow and quiet. Ask yourself—How can I keep this simple? Whatever this is, you've tried it, have established that it feels good, that you like it, and are getting good results. When you've established all of that, then ask—

How can I keep this simple so that I may keep it?

If you complicate it, chances are very good that you will not want it anymore. You'll have taken a nice simple concept that was working for you, and complicated it enough to turn it into something that is not working for you, and feeds those things inside of you that still thrive on chaos, emotional pain, and emotional pain cycles. That is always an option. You can always turn anything simple into something very complicated and make the chaos pervasive again in your life.

When you begin to feel chaotic, or feel yourself moving into a pain cycle and being triggered over and over again, stop and ask:

What about all of this is simple? What are the elements that are simple? How can I slow down, get quiet, and find what is simple?

You know what simple feels like. You know what chaos and complication feel like.

You don't make *everything* in your life complicated, but the things you've habitually made complicated have become engrained in how you view the world. When you are doing something that feels good and makes sense to you, that you continually feel drawn to, and that is creative and fulfilling, occasionally along the way, you may still experience some bumps in the road.

Challenges can come up all of a sudden and you think, *What is that? I don't even know what that is.* If there is a habit that has become ingrained, or if you have a history of creating chaos, be careful that you don't make chaos out of these challenges when they come to you. Don't immediately assume that the chaos is moving in, and that you've done something wrong, and that you must be sabotaging this great thing that was feeling good and that you were doing well with. Recognize that there are always going to be things coming to you that you don't want or understand at first.

This doesn't make them such bad events that they'll ruin everything. It just makes them different and means that you need to:

> Slow down, get quiet, explore, and find the
> simplicity in this thing that has come,
> because it's always there. *Always*. If you are
> quiet long enough and listen for that still,
> small voice no matter what comes to you—
> again, *no matter what comes to you*—you
> will find the simplicity that exists within
> that experience.

Your lives are very simple on every level. Part of learning about choice is understanding what to do with the simplicity. This is a process. It's doubtful that you will awaken tomorrow and say, "I'm utterly committed to simplicity and from now on every single thing is going to be simple, no more complication for me, thank you very much."

What you will do, along with all the other changes and beautiful things that you are doing for yourselves, is begin to shift your perspective about the people and events that come to you. You will begin to recognize, particularly in relationships, when other people are choosing chaos and complication over simplicity. All of a sudden, you will feel things viscerally, and very differently.

When you are in simplicity, there is a feeling of lightness, where you feel okay and don't have to go out and look for trouble. You just feel okay. There seems to be a slow and quiet rhythm inside of you.

When you are choosing chaos, or when you are in the presence of others who are choosing chaos, you start to feel tightness in your body, as if you are bracing for the onslaught of the energy of chaos. You begin to tighten internally and feel a deep heaviness.

One of the easiest ways to recognize this is when the mind begins to race. When your mind is going too fast (and you can feel when this happens), trust that you are definitely moving towards chaos, if you are not there already.

Just breathe and say, *Okay, slow and quiet.*
Quiet and slow.

If you can't immediately find the simplicity in the situation:

Go back and recall what is simple in your life in the now—What do I know is simple? When I go and work in my garden, I feel simple. That's simple. When I cook a nice meal for myself and I sit down and eat it, that's simple. When I play or listen to music, I feel simple. When I sit and meditate, most of the time, I feel simple Remind yourself of when you've felt simple. Then locate that feeling. When you feel the feeling of simplicity, everything else quiets and slows down. Your body will begin to vibrate at a

> different energy level, a simple vibrational
> frequency, and you will begin to be drawn
> to that same energy—the energy of
> simplicity.

The energy of simplicity within the event will begin to reveal itself to you, because you are vibrating at that same energy frequency. When you are vibrating in the energy of simplicity, you will find what you are seeking to interact with the outside world.

Unless one of you has decided to go live on a mountaintop tomorrow, then you have elected to live where you are and interact with the outer world. Consciously seek the vibration of simplicity for yourselves throughout the days and weeks ahead. If you do, you will find your energy of simplicity with others and the events that arise.

It may often seem that the better way to go is to use the mind to try to figure things out. You'll be going merrily along, when something happens that is new, or is presented to you in a way that you don't understand, or an emotion is evoked such as frustration or anger, and you have to choose a reaction. Generally, what most of you do when this occurs, is to look through your repertoire of solutions past; *Well, last year when I was faced with something very similar, what I did was...* and you start to think, *What do I know? What do I remember to do? What did I do before?*

Here you are, gorgeous, Spiritual beings, who are just learning to really let your lights shine, to treat yourselves with kindness and dignity, and to celebrate yourselves without a care in the world as to whether or not anyone else joins in the celebration, when you run up against old thought patterns. Here is the trick to continue to blossom:

You must begin to accept that *everything* is
new, every time. It's *all* new, every day. In
each moment, you can stop and say, *Wait,
must I slow down and get quiet?*

There is an element of practicality that must be observed. What I'm generally speaking of is the larger events that come into your life. When you feel that simplicity, then you're doing fine and you need not worry.

However, when something happens and you start to believe that your mind is going to take care of it, to dip into the past and remember what you did before, that's okay. Don't throw it out. All that you've done before can be used as a tool. The past is a fantastic resource. Don't get rid of it.

Give yourself a little time to get simple, to
feel the simple energy vibrating, and open
yourself to feeling that vibration in any
new situation, with this person or
experience, so that you can find your way
through it. Let your past contribute
information, but don't let it dictate your
actions in the present.

Look at simplicity like breadcrumbs leading you through any situation—don't look for an elaborate meal every few feet—just look for the trail of breadcrumbs. They're always there, and will lead you through with grace, with dignity, and with peace.

Don't believe the lie that your mind tells
you about simplicity, that it is boring. Your
physical body requires simplicity; simple,

live foods and simple movement. Your emotions require simplicity; feeling what you're feeling in the moment, not hooking into the past or an imagined future, or borrowing someone else's emotions to feed off of your own. Give yourself permission to feel what you feel in the moment that you are feeling it. Nothing could be simpler than that. Simple spirituality; to just go within to discover the God that dwells within you and then say, *Hey, I know you from all around me! I know you. You've been here all the time. I remember you.* Nothing could be simpler than to open yourself to the beauty within and the beauty that is all around you.

Two elements that work beautifully together, and help you maintain your vibration of simplicity are to focus each day, all day, on what you have, and to feel gratitude for those things.

Remind yourself each day, every day, all day, to focus on your present abundance with gratitude. Even if you get stuck on the same three things you're grateful for, over and over again, that's fine. Open yourself to making this a ritual throughout your day. Identify what you do have in the moment. For instance, when you laugh with a friend, and discover, *Ah, I have humor! How wonderful!* Then I want you to feel gratitude

for that humor. Then feel how much that
humor has helped to get you through life,
how important it has been to you, and how
much you love to laugh. It is very simple.

If you can focus your day on what you already have
and feel gratitude for it, then these two things will jump
start the *vibration* of simplicity because they are entwined
in the *energy* of simplicity. Whatever you radiate outward is
what comes back to you. All of a sudden what you have and
what you feel grateful for far outweighs what you imagined
you didn't have or didn't like or want in your life. All those
things become very minor, and many of them disappear
altogether.

You will find that you've gone weeks without thinking
or complaining about the things you don't have, missed out
on, or that the Universe didn't grant to you, because you are
filled with joy about what you *do* have. What you'll find is
that when you focus on what you *have*, it grows! You get
more and more and more. This is the basis of abundance.
Very, very simple.

It seems as if you focus on what you don't have and if
you drive yourself through ambition to obtain it, and if
you're loud enough and fast enough, it will be yours. Then
when you get it, it's fun for about five minutes and then it's
out in the trash. You're done and on to the next thing.

Slow down. Get quiet, and feel what is real.
Feel what is real.

Let everything come down to its basic elements. You all
are gifted enough and sensitive enough to feel it. You do not
need great practice in this. You've been able to feel
simplicity your whole lives. That's why you're so sensitive.

You've always felt the difference between simplicity and complicated chaos. Trust in simplicity. Question the chaos.

MEDITATION:

Sit comfortably, close your eyes, and as you breathe, focus on the wonderful air that gives you life, feeds the cells of your body, expands your mind, and facilitates your great emotions.

Breathe, breathe, breathe.

As you breathe, I'd like for you to call forth from deep within yourself a few things in your life that you feel are wonderful. Just focus on those things and feel the outcome of your focus as gratitude. Notice the good feelings that arise.

As you bask in what you have and feel gratitude, notice the simplicity that exists within you by using this simple exercise:

Take three deep breaths and on the exhalation, let go of the meditation.

Always remember, the more you vibrate with simplicity based in gratitude, the more you will serve yourself and your world. This is how you will change things for the better; one experience at a time.

Thank you for allowing me to serve you.

Namaste ~

CHAPTER 4
Complex by design

One of the first things Mother taught me directly, as well as through others, was to simplify my life. I found this baffling. Groucho Marx once said, "*A child of five could understand this. Send someone to fetch a child of five.*" I excelled in complicating my life. To an addict, simplicity is anathema. If high drama were not occurring, I felt naked and rudderless. I relished being deeply involved in my friends' complications. I happily climbed onto their emotional roller coasters and strapped in for the ride. After all, if I were focused on them, I didn't have to face myself.

Without knowing it, I had created a belief that if people needed me, then I had purpose. If they didn't, I was superfluous. Since people rarely did what I told them to do, even when they asked for my advice, manipulating them to take the advice provided a bottomless pit of complication. A part of me felt genuine in my desire to help others find a way out of their pain. But the part of me that was desperate to be loved knew I had to use the force of manipulation to twist others into doing things my way. The illusion of solving the problems of others was like a religion to me. It was years before I could even conceive that my purpose was simply to live *my* life—not *theirs*.

It was 1993 and I was a year away from knowing Mother Mary consciously. Most days, feeling and trusting my intuition was as rare as rain in the desert. As a result, whenever people spoke with authority, I would think, *Yes, this person knows. I will do as they say.* Some of that advice helped me heal and some did not.

Because I was not eating compulsively or starving, all the pain I had been keeping at bay for so long was coming up. For me, then and now, it sometimes feels as if there is too much pain; that I can't look at it all. I still need things to get lost in, because I'm afraid of facing myself completely. I can only do it a little at a time. With Mother's help, I don't reach for complication first when I feel lost, yet it still creeps in and starts to influence my choices.

Much that was happening in metaphysics at the time was perfect for me. It was cerebral, complicated, and advocated shortcuts. Many of the solutions promised I'd never feel pain again because there was no reason to, and if I *did* feel pain, it was because I wasn't doing it right; if I'd cut all my negative energetic ties then I'd be happy all the time. I thought, *Great, sign me up! I'm all about no pain. I've had enough to last ten lifetimes.*

Even though I'd found a deeply spiritual path which relieved my food obsession, I still wanted to avoid that path by finding an easier, less revealing way because it asked me to be open and willing to grow. I believed that being naked and exposed to others would result in their rejection of me. So I sought complexity, excitement, disembodied Spirits, and unobtainable goals like ascension.

I gravitated to teachers who told me to love myself, and go out and spread light. But just being told to love myself, didn't make it so. Again and again, I attached myself to people who told me *what* to do, but not *how* to do it. The frustration that came with repeated failures made me feel even worse.

It was like the well-meaning people I told about my eating disorder, who would say, *"Why don't you just try eating less?"* Eureka! Of course! Why didn't I think of that? The shame of being unable to stop overeating on my own burned inside me. My inner critic assured me that loving myself was one more thing I would never be able to do right.

My friend Cassy introduced me to Sean, a dark haired, dark-eyed man with a friendly smile that people naturally gravitated to. He fit seamlessly into our circle of friends. He was a channel and we were fascinated by his gift, and charmed by his kindness. It was my first experience with the phenomenon of channeling, and from the first moment I knew I had found something significant. He explained that he channeled a group soul or a collective consciousness that had finished all their lifetimes on earth, and had recombined into an entity that taught from another plane of existence, and referred to themselves as Michael.

Sean had been given four tickets to see the Dalai Lama at the University of Arizona in Phoenix. I knew right away that I wanted and needed to go. I didn't know much about the Dalai Lama and had never had much interest before, but a flare of intuition told me I had to be there. When Sean said he wanted to visit Sedona afterwards, I thought, *Why not? I love visiting new places,* but I really didn't feel much preference one way or the other. Sean, Cassy, and I ultimately decided to go.

That weekend felt like a crossroads for me; spiritual kindness or spiritual boot camp. I didn't see it at the time, but I was the hare, racing through everything looking for shortcuts that were dramatic and exciting.

I was amazed at how many thousands of people were jammed into the basketball arena at the university. The air buzzed with excitement. A small raised platform was at one end, opposite my seat, with two wooden chairs on it. Behind the platform, three slender, maroon banners with what looked like simple gold knot work symbols hung from the ceiling.

I was chatting with the man sitting next to me, when all

of a sudden I stopped talking mid-sentence along with thousands of others as the room fell silent. I looked down at the stage, and two men dressed in saffron and maroon robes stepped onto the platform. A kind voice announced, *Ladies and gentlemen, His Holiness the Dalai Lama.*

For me it was love at first sight. Never had one person affected me so dynamically. I had an overwhelming desire to hug him and adopt him as my grandpa. That night, he decided not to use his interpreter. I understood about one in fifty words and didn't care. For an hour and a half I sat smiling, filled with joy and contentment. Here was a stadium filled with the peace I had begun to feel during my own morning prayer time, that I still performed on my knees. I felt humbled, and was content to be there for as long as he was willing to stay. I know now he was offering us the path of kindness. His transcendent generosity made my Soul sit up and stretch as if it were awakening from a long sleep, not with blaring alarms, but with the soft kiss of true love that Sleeping Beauty received from her beloved. When he left, I was sad because I wanted to go with him and contemplated becoming his groupie.

Afterwards, at a local restaurant, we compared experiences. We were more animated than usual. None of us had understood a word the Dalai Lama had said, but we fell in love with him anyway. What to do with that love? That was a question without an answer.

The next day we drove North through the desert, passing tall Saguaro cactus plants and dramatic rock formations on our way toward Sedona. The stark open spaces framed by rock in more shades of orange than I knew existed, gave me a languid feeling. Time began to slow. The landscape stretched out before us with an open invitation to discovery.

Sedona was like nothing I had witnessed before. As we

drove over the last hill and into the Verde Valley, I had a sense of excitement, as if something were building with each mile we drove. The rocks in the valley ranged in color from intense rust-orange to soft faded pink. Growing up in Birmingham, Alabama, I was familiar with the red clay that comes from such high iron content in the soil, but to see it throughout the entire landscape was staggering.

We dropped off our things at a Motel 6 and went out to explore, wandering where our intuition guided.

That first night, we drove out to Boynton Canyon. The night was beautiful. The stars were abundant, and so close they made crowns for our heads. With no artificial lights, the vastness of the night sky in such a wide-open space filled me with the same wonder I felt at the beach. I had discovered the desert's ocean. The air was warm and smelled of sweet grass and promise.

Sean's car was a decidedly on-road vehicle and was unprepared for traversing the desert at night. When the rocks threatened to claim our oil pan we had to pull over and stop driving.

We were fortunate that the moon and stars provided enough light, since we lacked a flashlight, water, and apparently, common sense. We got out of the car and lurched around for a bit before we found a rock with a flat surface all three of us could sit on together. We sat down to commune with the rocks, animals, and Spirits of the land. I felt as though I were floating in nature's hands.

Within minutes, all three of us began receiving messages and images of beings from another planet. It was completely unexpected and energetically overwhelming. I felt as though I had grown enormous. My body felt partially numb as if my etheric growth spurt outpaced my brain's ability to comprehend my new size. I had been experiencing that exact feeling on occasion since childhood, but never knew why. It wasn't a painful feeling, nor was it pleasant, but it was familiar.

The clarity of vision I was witnessing inside my head insured I would never be the same.

I have always had a rich fantasy life, but this was different. Usually I don't visualize—I have a knowing of things—but now I was seeing full-color visions when I closed my eyes. I could see a room that was plain and unadorned, like a room in an office building that is rarely used. The being that stood before me in my mind's eye was dressed in a plain, muted gray jumpsuit. It looked human in shape and size. Its head was a little larger than the average human being, and a cloud or mist obscured its face. It was the only thing about my vision that was unclear.

This being was trying to communicate something to me with great urgency, but it was happening too fast for me to make sense of it. I remember feeling that there was too much energy in my body all of a sudden. I felt sweaty and my heart was pounding, as if I had consumed a line of cocaine. I noticed Cassy having a similar reaction. Our eyes flew open at the same moment, and we began talking over each other to try and convey to Sean what we were seeing and hearing.

We were all seeing and hearing a slightly different version of the same thing. Suddenly, having four walls and a door that locked seemed vital, so we decided to go back to our hotel room.

The drive back to the hotel was fast and frantic. Locked safely in our room, we huddled on the bed and faced each other with hearts pounding and sweaty hands clasped. We took turns sharing the images and information that was coming through us.

This was my first experience of being a channel. I was frightened in the way of something new. Will it turn out to be a kitten or a cobra? Along with the expanded feeling I have had since childhood, I sometimes sensed the presence of something else in my childhood room with me. It never felt malevolent, but I was afraid of it. I had no context in which to put it. We never talked of such things growing up; not because my parents didn't believe in it, just that it wasn't their experience. That night my excitement was laced with that same fear of the unknown. I felt placed on that imaginary pedestal of special, superior to others, very different than the humble serenity I felt in the presence of His Holiness, the Dalai Lama.

That weekend I had been offered two very different paths. One was to study with the Tibetan Buddhists, a movement that is based on peace through acceptance and forgiveness, much like the recovery group that was helping me stay sane with food. The other was exciting, full of fear, and seemed slightly dangerous. As an addict new to spirituality, which one do you think I chose?

My experience in Sedona that weekend overshadowed and minimized my experience with the Dalai Lama. This was the beginning of many years of choosing to grow through continued complications, rather than the joy of simplicity. Deep down I felt I deserved a hard life, so I had to keep choosing experiences that had a powerful element of struggle and complexity. I don't regret my choice because I use the past to learn from, so I can make better choices in the present. But it definitely lengthened my journey within.

Channeling in and of itself is certainly not a punishment. It is one of the best things that ever happened to me. But the way I was choosing to go about my life was punishing. Yet I see now that I was selecting a path that left me room to run away and hide when I needed to. I wanted it to seem thrilling and important with a little devotion thrown in. Mother says all paths lead to God, so I know I chose the right one for me.

We found out Sedona was hosting an earth healing weekend the following month, and vowed to return and bring reinforcements. Back in Los Angeles, we were pumped up and talked incessantly about Sedona and the extraterrestrials, with the slightest reference to the Dalai Lama. Since most of our friends were newly recovering addicts, they were salivating to jump into the thrill of meeting the mother ship and possibly hanging out with the Pleiadians.

When I first began my journey of conscious awakening, some wise people often told me not to leave before the miracle happened. For me, the miracle was that there really was no crossroads. Whether I sat with Buddhist monks or aliens, I would still be me, with all my cravings for complex emotional upheaval and a need to keep hidden so I could feel safe. The Dalai Lama planted seeds of himself deep within me, right alongside all the other seeds of wisdom given to me over the years. As those seeds sprouted, I learned the value of a simple life. Complexity and struggle were as temporary as I chose to make them. It was the path of simplicity and peace that ultimately called to my soul.

Kindness to others and myself, patience, forgiveness, and letting go of resentments were new to me and impossible to practice without Mother's help and direction. She broke everything down into actions and behaviors. She taught me how my actions carried more weight than anything else. Then and now, Her teachings encourage me to make the simplest choice when deciding how to behave. How could picking up the phone and getting support possibly get me to transform something as big as my fear of loss? How could sitting down with Her in meditation each day possibly help me surrender my fears more easily? Yet they did, slowly but steadily they did.

Simplicity is the energy I now embrace. It offers me a less painful day-to-day life. When complication overwhelms me and I want to run and hide, I grapple with it because I'm still me, but then Mother reminds me to let Her have it. If I'm not sure what the simplest choice is, She guides me to write in my journal, give and receive support, and spend time inside myself with honesty and compassion until I find my way. She gently reminders me that I don't have to do it all myself, nor figure things out right now. When I am willing to take simple direction from Her, the miracle happens. The complex problem unwinds itself from my mind and the solution becomes a series of actions to take in the moment that lead me exactly where I need to go.

CHAPTER 5
Trust

The next step in building a foundation of love in your life is the exploration of trust. Such a small word holds quite a big energy. Trust is one of the primary issues that you all struggle with. Again, and again, and again, I hear you say that you do not trust and cannot do this or that with your life or that you cannot move forward because you have deep problems with trust. When I have questioned you about your definition of trust, you have come back to me and said that to not trust is to not believe in something. So I asked the question again—*What does it mean to trust?* You responded that to trust is to completely open yourself up to something—to allow—to have confidence in something. Trust is believing in the truth, and then letting go. Some of you said that trust was a safety issue, and some said a faith issue; indeed, these are all correct.

> The word I would say that comes closest to
> defining *Trust* in its essence and feeling is
> confidence. This is a simple way of
> understanding what trust is because when
> you don't have confidence, you lack trust.

You would need to take the definition of confidence, or its meaning, and multiply it by one thousand in order to understand the energy that you put into the word *trust*. Confidence has a more casual feeling to it; but trust, for many of you, feels like life and death, do or die. The stakes are always very high when you talk about trust. Confidence can be lost and regained. It can get holes poked in it, and it can be repaired, but often times for humans, when trust is undermined or lost, it is never regained. Relationships are lost, countries go to war—so much happens due to trust, or lack of it.

Many of you know trust when you see it, but many times you do not. You miss it when you put your own issues on top of a very simple or basic understanding. For each of you, trust is different, unique. That's why there are so many different ways of seeing and feeling it. Something that is so important in your lives, and yet has so many different versions or meanings, can be difficult to manage. Your meaning of trust may be different from someone else's, and when there's a violation of trust from your perspective, it may not be by his or hers. What often happens between people or groups of people is that they're not all working from the same definition of trust, which will cause problems right from the start.

Most people do not take the time to define what anything means to them, and so use words or phrases just because they heard them growing up. By keeping trust vague and undefined, it can become twisted and used in all sorts of different ways.

For example, you may suffer from feeling not good enough, that you don't have enough money, or that you're not smart enough. So then my questions to you are, *"How much money is going to be enough? What must you know in order to be smart enough? What does it mean to not be enough?"*

Usually, people cannot define that for me.

The homework then, is to write down what *would* be enough, and get very clear about

> that. Then, all of a sudden, it becomes
> attainable. If it is always vague and
> undefined, you will never obtain it. Let me
> restate that so you understand its
> importance: *If you allow something to
> remain vague and undefined, you will never
> obtain it.* How could you? How could you?

The definition of trust will change as you grow. I'm not saying, however, that when you define something that it is set in stone. Your life is fluid and it will always be changing. But you are on the path of bringing darkness to light. To begin to understand what trust means to you is very important. Otherwise, if you do not, you will continue to use it as an excuse not to move deeper into relationships, not to be honest with Self, not to move forward, and not to obtain or move into the things that you say you want and need.

Trust is based on your life experiences, and this is how most of you define just about everything in your lives; but most importantly, this is how you define trust. You learn it from the beginning, from infancy. As you grow from infancy through to your adulthood, you learn that there are certain things in your life that were fulfilled, and there are certain things that were not. Depending on what you brought into this life from other lives, and depending on the type of personality you chose for yourself in this life, you will either focus on what was fulfilled, or what was not fulfilled. As you grow, this will not be a conscious choice. At one or two years of age, you do not suddenly wake up and think, *You know, I really want to focus on the negative things in life and how terrible it is. I think I'm going to just stay right here in this negativity for good.*

It is the people and events in your life that come together to create who you are, and how you perceive what happens to you.

> Throughout the next few weeks, I want you
> to give some thought to trust. Meditate on
> trust and what it means to you personally.
> Also, meditate on, and then ask yourself
> whether you feel any trust. Whom do you
> trust? Why do you trust them? What are
> their qualities that you feel make them
> trustworthy? Basically, I'm asking you to
> explore trust at all different levels and
> what it holds for you.

It is not the lack of trust that *creates* obstacles, but rather, it is the lack of trust that keeps you from moving *through* the obstacles. Often, lack of trust is the energy or element that is missing in order for you to take that first step out into the unknown, to do something new, or to take care of an issue that has been in your life for a long time. If you don't trust, it's very, very hard to take that first step; to have the confidence that the first step is going to get you somewhere, and it doesn't have to turn into another five year plateau. You must trust that taking the first step will lead you then to the next, and the next step, and the next.

Trust is something that must start with you. The essence of trust is truth, which is honesty of Self. You tend to place your trust in things and people outside of yourself. If you place all of your trust in a friend who has a different version or understanding of what trust is, so lives her life in her own particular way, then do you feel that she, or anyone, could carry the burden that you place on them? Please do not make the mistake of believing that it's not a burden. If you don't trust yourself, you will look to people and things outside of yourself to place your trust in.

Your version of *trust*, is really about *control*, because you want your friend to behave and react in a particular way depending on your hoped for outcome. Basically, you begin to have an image of your friend, of how she should behave or speak or act, and when she steps outside of that prescribed structure, you deem her untrustworthy. All of a sudden your trust is violated and you can't believe she would do that to you, how awful she is, and on and on. Whereas really, your friend was just being herself, and had no idea that you had created an entirely different construct of her.

When you trust *yourself*, your friend is then free to be and do whatever she wants, whenever she wants, and however she wants. How you perceive and react to her is up to *you*; not *her*. It's up to *you*.

You must go within to find trust of Self.

When you trust yourself, when you have confidence in yourself, when you are listening to yourself, all of a sudden the need to have others do what you want them to do and behave the way you want them to behave disappears, because the essence of your trust does not depend upon anything or anyone else except yourself.

When you are a child, you see things as a child. When people consistently do not do as they say they are going to do, particularly those who raised you, you tend to stop believing them. For many of you, this belief has been carried into adulthood and there is an expectation that people are not going to do what they say they are going to do. There is an energy inside of you that holds yourself back from communion with others, because you believe that they will disappoint you. So, how can you trust them?

This is one of those fears that you have carried over and turned into a pain cycle. It generates a lot of holding back and anxiety, and brings up doubts such as *I don't know if I want to get involved with this person, or these people, because what if they don't do what they say they are going to do? What's going to happen to me? How is that going to hurt my life? Better not to connect. Better just to stay safe.*

You have created a set of rules around trust that people must follow in order to stay in your life; if they don't follow, they don't stay.

In your exploration of trust, I'd like for you to look a little bit at your life as a whole; not just the significant things, but its entirety. All of you have gone to stores and purchased things with cash, and depending on your age, some of you have done it hundreds or thousands of times. How many times, out of all the transactions since were a little child to now, have you lost money? How many times has someone taken money and not given you the correct change? The odds are that it's fairly small. This is one example of how the world is predominately a trustworthy place, meaning that what you give is returned to you in honesty, in good timing, and in good faith.

Each of you has had significant experiences where a loss of confidence occurred, primarily with your parents. But also, if you look back at your childhood, you will find that the majority of your everyday needs were met. There is no doubt that some were not, but the majority of them were, otherwise you would not be here. You were given life. You were given everything that you needed to get right here, today, right now.

As adults, you must, during your exploration of trust, ask yourself: Am I making decisions based on the very few times my confidence was not kept in the whole of my life, or am I making decisions

based on the majority of times when it was kept?

Consider all the little things that make up your entire day—from having water to shower, to a home that's still standing, to air to breathe, water to drink, food to eat, friends in your life, a place to work, to interact—then look closely at what you are focusing on. Are you focusing on the very small, although significant, minority, or the vast majority of your experiences?

In your relationships, where you all tend to have the hardest time trusting, look at the day in and the day out. If you look at all the things that made-up (or make-up) your relationships, you will probably find that there was trust, confidence, and assurances that were made and kept every day, day in and day out, week in, week out, month in, month out. So when relationships end, it's generally not from a lack of trust—it's just an inability to continue to relate deeply enough to remain in relationship.

Then, you take that, and say that you cannot trust because your relationships never work out! True, you did not marry someone at age nineteen and die together in bed at one hundred, but what are you basing your belief on? It is a rarity when relationships end because of deep violation that happens from one to the other. Generally, it's just an unraveling, a lack of relating, that cause people to naturally move down different paths. Yet you take these experiences and put them into a jar labeled *cannot trust* without really understanding how you are defining that experience.

When you were younger and began getting into relationships, the hope was always that you would be together forever and live happily ever after until death do you part. This is part of your culture, and is encouraged in romantic relationships. But rarely do people sit down with themselves and ask, *"Do I really, really, want to be with someone for the rest of my life?"*

Most of you would answer *no* right off the bat if you were being honest, because there is that knowing inside of Self that understands who you are intrinsically as a person.

And then question number two, *"What does it mean to spend my life with one person forever, day in, day out, for the rest of this lifetime? What are their habits? What makes me crazy? What's okay with me? What will it mean to live day in and day out with one person, to me, as an individual?"*

> What I am trying to say about trust, is that
> you collectively expect a lot of it, without
> really understanding what you truly need.
> Trusting yourself, learning to understand
> yourself and your inner compass so you
> can hear what's inside and what you really
> feel is your task. When you know yourself,
> then you trust yourself.

Much of your mistrust does not come from outside, not even from your parents, because children are enormously forgiving. You can make mistake after mistake after mistake with children and they will always say, *"I love you, mommy. I love you, daddy. You're the best."*

Where your mistrust *really* comes from is in not trusting *yourself.* If I blindfolded you, put you in a car and turned on the ignition, and then I put your foot on the pedals and told you to *go*, but not to take the blindfold off, how far do you think you would get? Probably not out of the parking space.

When you are going blind from the inside,
you cannot feel where you're going,
because you are not listening.

You often want to immediately look outside of yourself for the answers and put the onus of trust on others (which becomes a burden to them). Then when you discover that those other people, institutions, or events can't lead you to the right place (because they are generally driving just as blindfolded as you are), you say that you don't trust the world, or God, or this person or that group, when really they're just doing and being what they're here to do and be.

When you learn to trust yourself, which comes through the practice of listening, you will easily find your inner compass. Base your trust in yourself, one day at a time. Remind yourself that you listened to yourself yesterday and it felt good and centered, and things went okay. You will slowly but surely begin to trust yourself a little bit more, and gain a little bit more confidence in self. Build on that each day; you are learning something new.

To live within is very new and not something that most of you were brought up to do. It's something that you are learning. Instead of thinking in terms of trust when you're in relationships, think in terms of what you need; if you need honesty in a relationship, then explain that to friends, family, or significant others. Tell them that you need complete honesty, and then, if at some point you find that's not happening for you, the relationship will have to be reevaluated, because you have determined that honesty is the most important thing to you (or whatever it is that is the most important thing to you). Take out the guessing and stop putting the burden of trust on others, unbeknownst to them. Let them know what is important to you so that you understand each other.

Trust is really just another word for honesty.

If you say to me that you are going to do something, and then you don't do it, you call that a lie in your culture. When you say that you are going to take the trash out and then you don't take it out, is it forgetting or a lie? Yes, you can forget, but it's still a lie, because in a sense you are putting something off, which opened you to the possibility of forgetting. You are committing to things and not following through. You are talking often about what you're going to do, and what you want to do, but when it's not happening, you forget how to trust yourself.

You have to be trustworthy—*you*, not anyone else. *You.* If you cannot be honest with yourself, and I mean deeply honest, please don't expect others to be so. That is unfair, because you are asking something of someone else that you cannot give yourself. Instead of focusing your trust on others or outside events, just let that go for a time, and really, really just focus on yourself. Ask yourself, *"Am I following through on the things that I'm talking about? If I say I am going to do something, and then I don't, what do I do about it? Do I go back and make amends and try to take care of it? Or do I just conveniently sweep it under the table and pretend it never happened?"* Go deep within and ask, *"Do I lie to myself?"* If the answer is yes, then you are violating your own trust.

If you struggle with trust issues, it is because you don't trust yourself. If you cannot trust yourself, you will not trust others, and you will not trust life. You will not trust that the universe is there, holding you no matter how many times you are in certain types of relationships, or how many times you change jobs, or make any other changes that might look similar to past changes you've made. In a broader sense, try not to focus on your fear of trust. Try to take each situation as new. Try to look at each relationship as new.

You learn from the past, but do not apply the past to the present. It will not fit. Each experience that you have is unique. If you try to define something in the present, according to what happened to you in the past, you will miss what you're in right now. Trust is really not an accumulation of facts and figures that have to go in a certain way. Trust is a feeling, not an emotion; the feeling tells you that you are on firm ground, standing on a foundation. Even if the house isn't built and you don't know how it's going to turn out, and have no idea where you're going, you still feel grounded, and that there is a solidness to what you are doing, or what you're participating in. *That* is trust. Let that be your guide. It's very simple. Learn from the past, but leave the past in the past. This is especially true for your issues around trust.

For the majority of you, it's impossible to know what's around the corner. That's life! It's impossible for you to predict with any great accuracy exactly what is going to occur tomorrow, or next week, next year, or ten years from now. You do not know completely all the experiences that your soul desires for you to participate in.

You can get lost in what your culture tells
you that you *should* be doing, or you can
stand firm in the knowing that whatever

you're doing is exactly what you're
supposed to be doing as defined by no one
but you. This is trust, and what you hold on
to.

Self-confidence is what you build *your* life on, because people will do exactly what they want and need to do for *themselves.* They'll say what they want and need to say, and they will confound you, frustrate you, make you laugh, make you love, and make you cry; usually, when you least expect it and in a way that you didn't anticipate. Put your trust in that—and trust, beyond a shadow of a doubt, that people are going to be exactly what they need to be, and so too are you—and when you do, all of a sudden, everyone has room to breathe and explore; room to be themselves.

Trust can't be defined or fulfilled by anything outside of you. If people are honest, and if honesty is important to you, then engage with them. Be in relation with them. If humor is important to you, and you find people who you find humorous, then engage with them, be with them. Understand what you need in order to relate peacefully with others. If you find people who need and practice the same things that you need and practice and you relate, commune, and connect with them, then be with them. If they don't relate, commune or connect with you, then don't be with them. Let it be that simple.

If you get lost in wanting others to be a certain way before you give of yourself, you will be waiting a long time to connect with that which you crave. Give of yourself freely, because you trust yourself. You know that each day, you are going to take the very best care of yourself that you know how to do. And if pain comes into your life, then you'll move through it and beyond it. If you base your present off of past pain, then you will never trust the cycles of life and relationships, or in the evolution of your own being.

When you trust yourself, you stop having to figure so many things out before you give of yourself or open yourself up to others, because you trust that you're going to be okay. You feel yourself. You feel where you're going and where you've been. You can feel the knowing that you are exactly what, where, how, when, and who you need to be.

When you can keep giving without guarantees up front, you learn to trust in life and to have confidence in knowing that life is a series of wonderful experiences; some painful, yes, but most joyful, interesting, exciting, and fun.

The last thing I want you to consider as you explore trust for yourself, is whether or not you are setting up a special set of expectations, that you save just for things that you feel require a great deal of trust. What is your set of guarantees that you look for before you are willing to just take off all of your clothes and jump into the deep end? What set of requirements do you set up again and again and again without even knowing that you're setting them up? Look for your checklist, and when that checklist is not met, make note of how you hold yourself back from life. And if safety is one of the things on your checklist, ask yourself, "How can I give that to myself? How can I let go of the need to have others provide that for me, or events to provide that for me, before I am willing to be a part of

things?" Or maybe, just maybe, you're
ready to take that checklist and just throw
it out.

MEDITATION:

Sit quietly and close your eyes. Place both feet on the floor. Feel your feet on the floor. Feel how solid it is. Feel how solid you feel in your body; how wonderful and strong your body is. With each breath, as you move more deeply into yourself, what does trust feel like for you? What is the essence of this energy? Breathe life into this energy of trust that is within you. Know that the more you trust yourself, the more you will trust Spirit. The more you trust Spirit, the more you will trust life. The more you trust life, the more you will trust love, which is the heart of all things. I encourage each of you to trust yourself just a little bit more, and to remind yourself that you make good decisions. On the few occasions when you don't feel that you've made good decisions, remind yourself that you have everything you need inside of you to make a better one. You have God within. You are courageous, strong, intelligent, wonderful, brilliant beings, worthy of trusting. Now breathe in what I just said to you. Breathe it in and let it settle within.

Now take three deep breaths and on the exhalation, let go of the meditation. You may open your eyes. I thank you for allowing me to serve you.

Namaste ~

CHAPTER 6
I was untrustworthy

One of the many things I love the most about Mother's teachings is Her focus on action and solution. Every time She comes through my body to teach, She leads us deeper into love, trust, forgiveness, and surrender. She comes at it from every conceivable angle, and at some point, speaks to each person's need to understand these sacred principals and how to awaken them within. She is always offering actions that will bring about the solutions to our difficulties. But that's the tricky part; will we do them? Not always.

The actions I took as a practicing addict destroyed my trust, and created wreckage that tore me apart mentally, emotionally, and physically. What I discovered early on in my spiritual awakening is the appalling lack of trust I had for myself. I had abused myself daily, placed myself in risky situations to be hurt, and ignored my needs for so long, that I had become untrustworthy.

Spirit began making itself known to me with greater frequency. My friend's support felt buoyant, as if I floated on the ocean current, held yet fluid. All that was wonderful but I had lost confidence in myself and didn't know how to show up for myself. What was there to show up for? Inside I knew I would continue to let myself down, just as I had done a thousand times before.

Too often, I'd say I would do something positive for myself, and then never followed through. I would feel excited and hopeful, like a child whose parent promised to spend the day with them, only to be crushed when the parent always found excuses not to show up. This was a hard truth for me to face. I continued to mask it by blaming others for being unworthy of my trust. Someone else was always at fault for why things didn't work out for me.

Blame has been a constant companion in my life. It eroded my trust in myself and in life, until I had very little left. My shadow reaches for blame when I perceive that things aren't going the way I think they should go. It surrounds me with a false sense of protection, as if blame could change past events and bring me what I want. It provides me with the illusion that I am being wronged, that others are at fault, and that I am the victim. The feelings of self-pity that came with that illusion made me feel trapped and smothered, like there wouldn't be enough of anything to help me to survive.

I had no idea how much blame and self-pity affected my ability to trust. Mother teaches that without trust, we will never feel safe. If I didn't feel safe, I wouldn't be able to trust. That was a bind I needed to get out of. She taught me that safety and security are the number one, most important elements for a happy, peaceful life. She helped me to see that I had to change my belief about safety in order to build trust.

My idea of safety was to keep the walls of my castle strong, build a moat, stock it with monsters, and have archers on the walls ready to defend me to the death. I made the people in my life swim that moat, fight off the monsters in it, climb my castle walls, and then I'd finally apologize after I had convinced them that they had wronged me. They often gave up on me from sheer exhaustion. Then I got to blame them for giving up on me.

My lack of safety and trust fed my blame. My blame fed my victimhood. The more I felt like a victim, the more I stayed behind my walls, afraid to venture out and encounter pain. The deeper my isolation, the less pain I felt from others, but it also kept me from joy and love.

Upon my awakening, trust was a faint whisper. Mother provided the grace of insight and the shift in perspective that I needed to build new beliefs. Staying away from sugar and binging was one of the hardest things I have ever done. Even knowing Mother was handling the vast majority of my recovery, I still felt as if I was carrying around an elephant.

On many occasions, I found myself cruising the cookie or ice cream isle at the grocery store, furtively looking around as if I were trying to score drugs, for no other reason but to contemplate eating something destructive. I felt poised on the knife's edge of indecision—*should I eat something sweet, or not*? Just when I would decide to do it, I'd look for the thing I wanted most, but the store would be out.

That moment gave me room to breathe, and in that breath a tiny bit of trust was born. I was able to step back and think, *not today*. I became aware that those kinds of things were happening to me all the time. A spark of belief began to glow inside me that something was supporting my new actions. I thought I needed God for the big things in my life because my pain felt so big. But Mother became the god of small things for me, and it turned out to be what I needed the most.

I hadn't realized that my life was comprised of millions of small decisions, rather than just a few big ones. I began to hope that if Mother was supporting me in all the everyday choices, then She would be there when the big ones happened as well. Over the last two decades, that hope became fulfilled until Mother became the god of *all* things for me. I built my trust one small miracle at a time. Every time a store was out of my chosen binge food or a friend would call to offer support just as I was heading out to buy binge food, or I would say a small prayer and the need to overeat would lift, with every one of these events, I further built my foundation in trust.

I was having trouble keeping a job and was behind on my rent. I remember sitting on the dingy, blue striped couch in my living room, home to many of my binges, and crying as a friend held my hand. He looked me in the eye and told me that as long as he had a place to live, that I had a place to live. The gift of home he offered gave me an even bigger space in which to breathe.

Safety is still the number one item on my checklist that I need to feel before I jump into life.

Support from the divine, friends, and to some extent, the community, must be present in order for me to step into the unknown, which basically comprises all of life. I have discovered I do not do well on my own. If I have clamped down control on something and won't let in light and air, it never goes well.

When Mother came into my conscious awareness about a year after my spiritual awakening, I fell in love with Her right away. I fell for Her hard, like my attempts at ice-skating. One minute, I'm up and gliding forward, the next I'm pin wheeling my arms, my ice skates are where my head should be, and I'm flat on my back, dazed and breathless. I was dumbstruck when I realized that I'm at my best when I'm connected to Her, body and soul. She slowly became my new definition of safety. At first I was terrified. My connection to Her was an invitation to intimacy and co-creation, not just with Her, but with everyone. That was a party I didn't want to attend. I really wanted to hit Her over the head and drag Her back behind my castle walls so I could feel good and stay safe the old, familiar way.

She coaxed me to send the archers on the walls home, set free the beasts in the moat, and dismantle my castle, stone by stone. Twenty-one years later I'm still working on those stones. Sometimes I turn them into thousand pound boulders that I think will crush me if I try to move them, but with Mother's help they become pebbles I enjoyed skipping across the moat.

When I try and do things alone behind my castle walls, I get almost nowhere and fear paralyzes me. I procrastinate and lose my way. But when I'm willing to collaborate, even a little, with Mother and those around me, I feel focused on moving forward and want to show up for whatever is in store for me.

For every miracle of support and every moment of communion with Mother, my trust grows. It has become a living, breathing thing inside of me, alive with purpose and strength. It allows me to feel that no matter what is happening in my life, it will be okay, and I'll be all right. It seems like such a small thing as I look at what I've written on the page, and yet for me, it was and is Earth shattering. This feeling didn't emerge until eight years into my spiritual life. I worked hard for it. Unconsciously, I knew I needed it to survive.

Eleanor Roosevelt said, *"You must do the thing you think you cannot do."* She was right. I never thought I would feel safe enough to trust myself and the rest of the world as I did when I was a child, but Mother knew. She came to me first as dolphins, then an angel, and finally as Divine Mother; each a form I could accept at the time, and which opened me to trading my old ways for new ones.

CHAPTER 7
Heart energy

On the pathway to love, we must take the time to explore your heart. It is here that love is at its most powerful within you. I'm going to use the seven chakra system to help explain the energy of love within your heart center, or heart chakra. Your heart chakra is the place that is associated with love, and referred to as your love center. There are three chakras below the heart chakra, and three above it. The heart chakra, the fulcrum on which the lower and the higher chakras are balanced, is in the center. The three lower chakras—the root chakra at the base of the spine, the emotional chakra located in the lower abdomen, and the third chakra or soul center located in the solar plexus—are the chakras that are most predominant in humans. They energize, encapsulate, and hold your humanity within them.

The three higher chakras above the heart—the throat chakra, third eye chakra, and crown chakra—elevate you from the basic aspects of humanity. The throat chakra is the seat of communication and self-expression. The third eye is there for your intuition and wisdom, and aids in your thinking and decision-making. The crown chakra serves your abilities to be fully connected spiritually.

There in the center of your chest, trying to balance it all is your heart center, the fourth chakra, holding the place between physical and etheric, between human and Spirit. It is this place within where you begin to discover your own divinity. It is this heart center that creates the knowing, the experience, of being Divine. This fourth chakra allows you to connect the physical and the non-physical.

When humans speak of love, it can be a rather confusing subject. You love a person, and you love pizza. You use the same word to describe an enormous variety of feelings and experiences, because it's hard to understand love. You've all been trying to define it for a very long time. There's a great desire to bridge the gap from human to divine in your feeling Self, and your everyday life. You can feel bogged down and burdened by your own humanity at times, and by your feelings of frustration, loneliness, and heaviness. All these things can be an impetus for wanting to transcend the physical, to grasp the spiritual, and to be a part of something bigger, something greater.

For some of you though, there is something much more taking place within you and your life. There is a knowing that, yes, you may have all these difficulties in your human life, but you are beginning to truly feel, even if it's only on an intuitive basis, that you are more than just the day-to-day feelings you have. You are more; not out there in Spirit, but inside your body. There is more to you than you might realize in this moment. There is more depth of feeling. There is more depth of creativity. There is more that you crave to understand, to experience. And though some of that is about what's out there in the world, more is about what's inside.

Your heart chakra, your love, is the bridge from the normal day to day to something higher, something more, something expanded within you. I feel that each one of you, in a form unique to yourself, desires more within the heart, and a stronger feeling of this bridge; a day to day knowing that you are Divinity now, as you are.

You don't have to go out and make big changes. You don't have to be something other than who or what you are now, in this moment. The Divinity is within, for the evolution of the individual. You don't become Bodhisattva by changing everything about yourself. You become Bodhisattva when you simply awaken to what is.

That awakening takes a bit of time, perseverance, and lots and lots and lots of patience. But your heart is engaged from the very beginning of your life to the very end. It is the part of you that is always gathering other hearts unto it. It is that part of you which craves connection, friendship, lover relationships, marriage, children, and pets—even goldfish!

Love is the desire to draw to you that which you can connect with to feel the same energy—the mysterious force that you all look for all the time. *All the time.* You want to love yourself, you want to love each other, you want to love your work, and you want to love your home. Always, you are striving to feel love. It is worth paying attention to a force that is so important to you, that you spend your lives seeking it in everything you do. Whether it's pizza or people, you want to love it.

Some people are very serious about their love of pizza; what does it give them? A joy, a feeling... It brings about a *feeling.* That feeling can be comfort, safety, contentment, or any number of positive feelings. Something happens inside of you when you give to yourself, connect with, and are conscious of love. When you are conscious of love and bridge the human/Divine experience, it is the heart that makes them one; it is the heart that takes the human and Divine and awakens them to each other so that they are no longer separate. They become one seamless experience.

One of the first steps to awakening is synchronicity. When you are aware of synchronicity, you are aware of love. You all equate synchronicity with things working out, and may think, *Well, I went there, and it showed up, and then that happened, and she called, and then it all just came together!*

Just like that, it comes together. Synchronicity is a feeling of the gathering of energy to create an event, an experience. When it happens with flow and with ease, there is a buoyant, expansive feeling that is always love.

Begin to expand your definition and understanding of love. Love connects the three chakras below the heart with the three chakras above the heart. *As above, so below.* It is the heart that brings it all together. Your definitions of love are often unconscious. Declarations are made without feeling. Be careful of this.

> Love is your most important energy as a
> human being. Without love, you cannot
> live. Even if you get food and water and all
> the rest, without the energy of love, you
> cannot survive. Love brings you back to the
> body and the physical plane, over and over
> again. Love makes the wheels go round.

At the end of this chapter, I will teach you a meditation to energize the heart chakra and how to use it as the connecting point for uniting it with the other six chakras. Once you learn the meditation, you may take a moment to use it in your daily experience.

> Start to think about your life, all the dots—
> go here, do this, do that, have this or that
> experience. Stop and take a moment before
> you get in your car, go to work, run errands,
> or do any of the many things, large and
> small, that you do every day—stop and ask,
> *"How can I connect with the energy of love in
> this situation, at this time, with these people?*

Where is that energy?" Continually asking yourself these questions will create a momentum that will awaken your whole being. It's easy to take love for granted, to forget about it, to not consider it when you make decisions and choices. If you were to think about every choice you make, and ask, *"How can I find love to connect with? How can I connect with love?"* instead of wondering about the outcome, or what you can get, or how you can make something happen, or how to control a situation, person, or activity, say to yourself, *"I'm going into this because I want love. I'm going to do this to feel love, and to find love. I'm going to energize my heart chakra when I go to sleep at night, when I wake up, when I eat food, when I interact with others, when I do my work, when I'm creative, when I make love, when I dance. I'm dancing for love. I'm working for love. I'm sleeping for love. I'm eating for love."* Keep this in the forefront of your being without deciding what love is ahead of time. Once you decide what form love is going to take in the situation, it becomes limited; very, very limited. You've gone from discovery to decision before you've had the experience. Knowing that this is the most powerful energy, and that it is responsible for connecting, awakening, and bridging everything in your life, would *it not make sense to explore your life from that energy, as an explorer with the desire for discovery would? What does love feel like here? What does it feel like with this person? What does it feel like as I sit and try to make this choice that is before me?*

You have these energy centers for a reason. They are meant to be in alignment for a reason. An elementary way to look at this is to imagine that these energy centers located on your torso, neck and head are designed to create gateways for psychic experience and communication, sexuality, creativity, and emotional flow. Gateways are to assist you in getting to know your own soul. And your arms and legs are there to carry it out. Imagine your torso and head as the receiver, and your arms and legs as the doers of the body. You are designed to receive energy in whatever form, whenever you wish.

You all want balance in love, work, life, and play. When you are in balance, you feel strong and that your foundation is good. Love is the energy that balances the two strongest aspects of your life; the physical and the Spirit. There is really nothing else. In this moment you are Spirit made physical. It is your judgment of love and how you define it, as well as your beliefs about love, that often do not allow you access to the full spectrum of what is possible within you. Love takes many, many forms. Be open and inquisitive. Place the energy of love within the consciousness of all that you do, without defining it; just *feel* it.

You can feel love, but it's very difficult to put it into words, despite what language you speak or how many languages you speak. You can come close, but you cannot quite really define it, not completely. There's a reason that words will always fall a little short of the experience itself, and that is because your experience is unique. Once you put it into words, the experience becomes more permanent, more general. When you trust the feeling that for you is love, when you let that be your guide regardless of the situation, the more balanced, connected, and plugged in you will be.

Your physical heart is responsible for a lot within your body and a lot within your life. Your life is dependent upon your heart, and it affects your whole body, all the time, in every moment. It is flowing energy through your body. The blood that moves in your veins and arteries is the energy that is always flowing, always moving. Your heart—love—is never static, never still. It is always creating. It is that which brings Spirit into the physical, and turns the physical back into Spirit. It is the bridge. Always moving, always creating—just as *you* are always moving, always changing—it is a reflection of the whole.

Your heart chakra is about that movement. It is seeking other heart energy, and propels you forward, encouraging you to try something new, to meet someone new, to reach out, to take a chance. In many ways this is where your courage comes from; your heart. Why else would you take risks over and over again? Reach out for love again even when you've lost it? Even when you've felt rejection, even when your love has been abused or criticized, still you reach. Still you risk. Still you move. You cannot do otherwise, because as humans you must have love. The energy has to flow, which is what brings me to the point of expressing to you in the simplest terms possible:

You cannot avoid love.

You cannot avoid the risk that comes with love, with reaching out again and again, even when your heart feels heavy. When there is sadness and grief, it's very hard to stay separate from love and push it away. It's exhausting, because it goes against your natural inclination.

You are designed to love in all its many
forms. And you are designed to receive love
in all its many forms. No matter how many
times you believe it didn't work out the
way you wanted it to, in reality, it worked
out *exactly* as it needed to work out. But
that is not always easy to accept.

What I'm asking you to consider, even if it's just for a little while, is how you can explore your love energy. To not take it for granted, and really get to know what that feels like for you. How it moves and works in certain situations; how often you deny it; how often you just forget about it, don't look at it, or don't pay attention to it because, *What if it doesn't work out?*

It seems odd that your highest spiritual chakra, your crown chakra, should be on your head, and your second highest, your psychic center, should be right through the brain, the mind, the mind that talks you out of love, *every time*. Odd placement when one is trying so hard to reach Divinity, and the mind just won't be quiet. Only the energy of love can break through the repetitive, more reptilian mind, into the higher aspects of your mind, and the parts of your brain that have the capacity to be aware of, and experience Spirit, and then translate that experience through the body, into your being.

This is where you find your balance. This is where you find the true meaning of all your experiences. Your heart is what leads the way to every person, every situation, you experience. It's what moves you to try again. It's what finally convinces you that no, you cannot isolate yourself;

no, you cannot live without love; no, you must not ignore friendships; no, you cannot skip meditation. You have to commune, commune, commune, because at the heart of love, you will always find communion. Connection. This is how you live. You connect. You commune.

> Without connection with each other, with
> yourself, with God, there is nothing.
> There is no life.
> So, as you go about your day, when you
> make decisions, when you think of your
> life, feel your heart center. Feel where it's
> leading you. What is it asking of you? Why
> are you being led in this direction at this
> time?

Because there is love. There is love, there is love, there is love. The more you open yourself to it, without defining it, the more you will know it's there; you will feel it. It is that which brings you to everything you are, everything you have, and everything you know. It draws you in. It leads the way. The more conscious you are of this energy, the more you immerse yourself in it, the more you consciously let it lead the way, the more balanced your life will be. When there is balance, there is ease, there is grace, there is simplicity. No matter what your life looks like on the outside, inside it will feel simple.

Each chakra can be used in your life. Many people sit and cleanse them, they try to balance them, but not many people try to actually use them. Yet that's what they're for. They are to be used and called upon to move the energy within them. When you say, "*I'm going to set my intention,*" that's where it comes from. Depending on the intention that you're setting, one of your energy centers fires up and gets going. Just like when your mind says, *"Pick up the glass,"* and then your arms move, hands move, fingers move; the message is sent. Think of your chakras as your tools. They're yours. Explore them. Yes, cleanse them. Wonderful. Balance them. Fantastic. But even better, *use* them!

Your chakras are designed for you to use to help your body and your life. They are energy centers, gateways. Go within them. Consciously explore them. They have great power for you. They are there to help you with creativity, with emotion, with feeling your soul, understanding your own Divinity through communication, regardless of what kind of communication it is—verbal, psychic, written, or emotional—it doesn't matter. They are there to help you both psychically and spiritually.

If you lead with the heart, with love, as you feel it in the moment, you might find that all your other chakras are firing up to give you more energy, and to help you to feel, on a more continual basis, your own Divinity.

I know that it is a challenge day to day not to get lost in all that is around you, clamoring for your attention. It can be overwhelming and confusing. Sometimes when you feel the burden of your own humanity too much, like an animal you'll desire to curl up, to protect yourself, to withdraw. It is always your heart that reminds you to unfurl, to blossom again, to reach out, to try, to flow. It is that which is inside of you that says you cannot stay stagnant. You cannot stay isolated. You have to reach out to live. You have to connect to life.

I suggest you try helping it along a little bit, by being encouraging of your own heart and recognizing it for all that it does for you. Really make a conscious effort to allow it a freer rein. Try not to deny it quite as much, but rather allow it more room to do what it is designed to do, which is to expand your life. This is love. Always, it expands, and never collapses.

MEDITATION:

Sit comfortably and close your eyes. Allow your spine to be nice and vital. Take nice, deep breaths. Fill your lungs and diaphragm fully, taking in more air than you normally would, so that on the exhale you really feel a letting go.

Reach your arms over your head, stretching them up. Exhale out the fingertips and wiggle your hands and fingers. Relax them down and rest them at your sides. Begin to settle into your heart as if you are relaxing with an old friend.

Now, begin to breathe in and out of your heart. With each breath, feel the energy, the gateway—however you experience it—feel it expanding. Allow it to expand.

Using your breath and your intention, take some of that expanded energy and move it down through your solar plexus, your belly, into your pelvis. Awaken the root, the hara, and the solar plexus, your soul center, as if they were becoming one with the heart chakra, melding four chakras into one.

Once again, using the breath and your intention, imagine your heart energy flowing into your throat, third eye, and crown, infusing and encompassing the higher three chakras. So now, seven have become one.

One chakra. One gateway. All that is Divine. Allow love to activate your sexuality, your creativity, your emotions, your connection to your soul, your communication, your psychic awareness, and your etheric Self. Allow this energy to awaken, to enliven, to strengthen, to support, to lead, to nourish, to expand.

Stay focused. The energy is yours. Claim it. Embrace it. Allow it to flow, as is natural.

Stay focused. You don't have to understand it. You don't have to figure it out. All you need do is feel it. Feel its natural state of flow, connection, and communion.

This is the power that is inherently within you. It's yours to do with as you choose. To direct as you choose. It is only in the denial of it that you feel lost, disconnected, and alone. Allow the saturation and the emergence of this energy that is always within you, as therein lays connection, balance, freedom.

Take three deep breaths, and on the exhalation let go of the meditation.

Go to your knees and place your forehand on the floor and relax into child's pose, grounding your energy. You may slowly sit up and open your eyes.

Now just imagine going through your day like that. How lovely.

Here is my suggestion: Just like you put on your clothes, call forth your love. If you call forth your love before you leave your house, every day, or as you get out of bed, or while you're dressing, you can make it a routine; to just take a moment—it doesn't have to be a big meditation—but just a moment, to feel the love. Not define it, not think about it, but *feel* it. Drop into it just for a moment and bring it forth into your day, into your consciousness. Do it again at lunchtime. And just for good measure, do it again before you go to bed. *Let me sleep in love tonight. Let me awaken in love. Let me eat in love. Let me just be in love today.*

That doesn't mean that you have to be happy all the time. That's not what love is. Don't define it. Let it be what it is for you. This is very important. Not anyone else's idea of love, but what it feels like inside of you. You don't have to name it, you don't have to understand it, but I do encourage you to feel it and to let it be more a part of your conscious, daily living. I promise you, you'll have a lot more fun.

Here is the warning label that I'm going to stick on this whole thing; if you call forth love, if you choose that energy as the guiding force of your day, you will connect—you will commune deeply with your own life—so if that's not what you want and you stumbled upon this completely by mistake, then disregard all I've said. Trust that you have arrived here on purpose. Of all the nights and days of the year, you came upon this today. Trust your own wisdom, and your own Self for bringing you here.

I thank you all for allowing me to serve you.

Take what you've been given and give it away freely, and there will always be more for you.

Namaste ~

CHAPTER 8
Heart and soul

Rumi says, *"Your task is not to seek love, but merely to seek and find all the barriers within yourself that you have built against it."* I suppose like most people, I took the love I was born with for granted. I loved my family and friends and they loved me. I never thought about that love or tried to define it. When my father died I became terrified my mother would unexpectedly die. My fear morphed into anger, and then she could do nothing right; it didn't help that I had officially become a teenager with my newly awakened hormones pinging around inside, lighting me up like a pinball machine.

I didn't have the skills to be grateful that my mother was alive. I could only fear her death. Experiencing so much loss in such a small period of time had caused me to collapse in on myself. Without making a conscious decision, I found myself distancing myself from others. On the outside, I continued to be as affectionate as I had always been—I laughed as much and tried to find the positive in any situation—but I couldn't manage a truly deep connection. I was wildly happy with new friends, but when they left my life, I never allowed myself to miss them or mourn their loss.

Countless relationships withered and died over the years, because I either attracted people who could only tolerate a certain amount of intimacy, or I fled from those seeking more. I blamed them, and went on to the next relationship. When it came to romantic relationships, my defenses killed it every time. Of course there were other factors, but the relief I felt when they ended was a common thread.

How then was I to be a vessel for Mother Mary's unconditional love and infinite compassion? How could I live Her grace, when every teaching ultimately centered on intimacy and communion with all life through love? Being new to channeling Mother, I twisted myself up in knots over these questions, and made myself so crazy that I wanted to pull my hair out by the roots, She would say, with a smile in Her voice and all the patience ever created, *"Beloved, all I ask of you is to be open and willing, the rest will come in time."*

Oh...

Incredulous, I proceeded to wallow in my doubt and stomp about deciding it couldn't possibly be that easy. I wanted to know now how I could be the ultimate shining example of Mother's light. How could I dazzle others with my wisdom when I was still so deep in my shadow? I was convinced I would disappoint everyone with my flaws and that no one would want to attend my channelings.

I lived in Sedona, Arizona at the time when a lot of my early channeling chaos was happening. My roommates and I lived in a neighborhood of ranch homes filled with retirees, strict neighborhood rules, and coyotes. I ran early most mornings, before the temperatures reached scorching highs that made me doubt my mother's lifelong assurance, that since I was not made of sugar, I wouldn't melt in the sun.

It was 7 am when I left the house wearing my running shorts and an old t-shirt, the sun warm on my skin. My running shoes, covered in red rock dust from my hike the day before, pound the smooth pavement. I ran past the perfect houses, with all the cars parked neatly in their garages. It felt like Stepford Wives meets retirement village.

The homes are cradled in spectacular, giant red rock formations under blue skies and clean air. I had become so used to sucking in the brown air of Los Angeles that my lungs were still getting used to the change. I ascended steeper roads, steadily running toward my destination. I liked to take different routes to get there, because I read once about the importance of not getting into a rut.

I stretched my long legs out on the last steep incline, ponytail slapping my neck. Halfway up I could see the square top of the chapel peeking through the mesa it was built into. The rock formations surrounding it reminded me of my childhood activity of dribbling wet sand into a lumpy, narrow pile on the beach.

My destination was The Chapel of the Holy Cross. I discovered this treasure soon after moving to Sedona. It is Catholic in faith, but open to all. It's the place in town that made my heart sing the loudest. I ran to this sacred site almost every morning before it opened to the public. The custodian and I had a silent agreement between us and he looked the other way for my early morning visits.

The walkway from the parking lot turned an elegant spiral up to the front doors of the chapel. The doors were already thrown wide open to catch the cool breeze on its way out of town. The day promised to be another scorcher. My heart was still pounding from my run and I could feel its beat all the way to my toes. As I approached the doors, something long asleep began to stir inside me. It was devotion and I was in awe of it. I went to meet my beloved Mother Mary, as I did each morning; the anticipation lifted me up and carried me inside.

The custodian looked up and we smiled and nodded to one another as he vacuumed the dirt off the carpet left by the hundreds of visitors that were there the day before.

The love in my heart swelled and I felt my being reach

out to touch Mother's presence. It seemed as though it came straight from a source deep within the rock itself, making this place feel holy to me. She pulled me to Her, as if by a force that was more potent than anything I had ever known, until I was sitting in the first pew, focused on the sculpture of Mother Mary before me. The artist Marguerite Brunswig Staude had created this sculpture of Mother Mary. She was the woman who designed and commissioned the building of the chapel as well.

Tears streamed down my face as if they cleansed and anointed me, body and Soul. I was alive in the glorious moment, and for the first time since childhood I feel a deeper sense of belonging to the Divine and myself.

The statue was only about two feet tall. The base rose up from behind to form the robe that rested on Her head. She was silver and gray in color, and looked to be on Her knees. With only the suggestion of facial features, She stared out at me and seemed to be looking at the infant laid before Her at the same time. Her hands were placed over Her heart as if in wonder; not because it was the Christ child, but because it was Her son. Everything about this sculpture was an invitation to joy. As I sat before Her, I imagined Her holding me with that same sense of wonder, because I am Her daughter.

As I sat and meditated in Her presence, I felt the walls around my heart cracking and crumbling. The love I kept trapped within rushed forward in joy. The custodian had turned off the vacuum and gone downstairs. I was alone in the silence that brought with it a stillness that was new to my busy mind and anxious body.

The swell of power within this sacred place nourished me in a way that nothing else had up to that moment in my life. Mother called me back to the chapel each morning, so I could continue to discover the communion that flowed between our hearts. I was filled with love. I was filled with gratitude and went to my knees at the foot of Her pedestal. She had reawakened my heart and I felt the willingness to return the next day for more.

My run home was expanded and light. My feet barely touched the ground. Devotion flowed through my veins and for a few minutes of the day I didn't fear the force of it or wonder where it would take me.

The chapel held space for me to explore intimacy and communion. Each day I dismantled my castle's defenses a little bit more than the day before. The simple act of sitting there gave me a glimpse into the power and majesty of the Divine and made it easier to commit my life to Mother. Not because it was what I should do, but rather what I needed to do for my own fulfillment.

After leaving Sedona, and what I came to think of as *my* chapel, whenever my fears and doubts insisted on running my life, in my mind, I went back there, and my heart settled and opened to love. It may not always be enough to quell the fear completely, but it's always enough to keep me going forward. Mother provides the simple way into my heart and into love—if I let Her.

CHAPTER 9
Forgiveness

Now that you have compassion for your dark night, you've embraced simplicity, learned to trust in yourself, and are willing to give love free rein, it's time to forgive your past within the present. Forgiveness is the key to enlightenment. I sometimes refer to it as the *art* of forgiveness, because in some ways, the development of this way of life is an art form. It takes creativity, it takes dedication, and it takes an honoring of the work itself in order to move forward on your path of consciousness.

Forgiveness is one of those things that sounds wonderful, but is often very hard to achieve or to feel, to really know that you are forgiving, or that you are being forgiven. It is a deeper spiritual truth because at the heart of it lies the essence of God—what you call love—in its purest form. It is a form that exists without judgment. To truly live in the energy of forgiveness is to live without judgment.

Judgment is one of the great human practices. You all do it for a variety of reasons. At the real heart of it, you judge because you need to feel safe. Judgment—before consciousness, before your search for God—is a way to feel safe. We belong to this group over here and we have this structure, this format, and this set of beliefs that define us as a group. And there's a group over here, and over here and over there, and everyone has a set of beliefs and judgments that create the structure of that group. It helps you to have a sense of community and safety.

Judgment is not a bad thing; it's not a bad habit. But, if you are seeking consciousness, if you are seeking enlightenment, then judgment tends to get in the way because those two things are at odds with one another. Enlightenment is about a state of curiosity. It is a state of openness. You cannot come to greater consciousness if you are not curious about life and everything and everyone in it. When you are *certain* about life, you can only go so far. If you know something to be just so, where is the room to grow? Where can you open in that? How can you blossom within that?

The need for judgment is completely understandable. If you do not have a connection with the Divine, if you do not commune daily with the Divine, then the need for judgment is paramount to your ability to go out into a very violent, uncertain world, and feel okay, and be happy, and create a life, and have children, or a career, or whatever it is you choose to do out in that world.

With judgment, inevitably, someone must be right and someone must be wrong. If the judgment is that something is bad for you or bad to do, and someone is out there doing it, then you determine that they are wrong. As humans, you enjoy being right. This is where your tendency towards self-righteousness comes from; the desire to be right rather than happy. You would pursue rightness to the gates of hell and back, waving a banner the whole way.

What happens when you decide that someone is right and someone is wrong is that you feel okay to blame whomever you have judged to be the wrong one. The energy around being *wrong* is a powerful burden for anyone to bear. When you blame, whether you are blaming only an individual or a whole group of people, or whether an entire group of people are blaming *you*, someone ends up carrying the burden of being wrong. Take for example, those in your society who commit murder. If you read about that in the paper or see it on television, even if they live across the country, you feel judgment, that they are *wrong*, and you blame them for the pain they have caused to the family and everyone that was involved. So in some ways, the collective can blame a single person; and of course, the more *wrong* the crime, the bigger the blame.

Someone like Hitler will be blamed and judged to have been in the wrong for hundreds of years to come, because he is a part of your collective history, and you all like to look at the past, over and over again, and then discuss it. So this one soul is going to carry a great burden, a very great burden. Throughout the history of humankind, there have been people who did things like this, and all of you have had lifetimes of darkness and participating in this type of thing as well. With the service you do in this life and other lifetimes, you begin to work off your personal blame, as well as the collective blame. This is the point, or the inception, of karma and reincarnation, because you all require the structure of judgment and blame. Karma provides you the key out of that box.

If indeed each person is deserving of God's love equally, then there has to be a way for people like Hitler to work their way out of that burden and the blame that stays with that soul until the soul can release it, not only for the individual, but also the collective. It has to be released. When you do something philanthropic, of service, then the collective says, *"Look what she did, how wonderful, how giving, how selfless."* This assists your soul in releasing the blame and burden that you carry from past lives. The collective is also releasing you from that burden that the collective holds and carries for each individual soul. There's a lot of blame out there.

When you blame, you cannot forgive. Blame is what always stands in the way of forgiveness, which is why forgiveness is not something that just happens. A little bit, at first, yes, but it's a process. Just like every other aspect of enlightenment, it is the process that brings you forward, one step at a time.

When you are blamed, or when you are doing the blaming, you create an energetic burden for yourself to carry, and for the person you have blamed to carry. For those of you who have been with me for a little while and plan to continue, you will find that what is coming through this body will become more and more subtle. What I am bringing forward are deeper issues for you to address as an individual, because it is my feeling that those of you that are here, those of you that continue with me, are choosing to hold a very specific energy for this planet. Your collective is changing, and things that have been tolerated for thousands of years will no longer be tolerated. In some ways, you all are at the forefront of these changes.

To see the subtleties in energy, and understand how you can use it well, first you must realize how powerful you are as individuals. When you read the account of that murderer in another state and you feel blame arise in you, you must be aware that you are adding to the burden of the collective. It's a choice. Because of the shift and what is happening on your planet, no longer will you get away with making choices without paying attention.

Basically, the energy that has already arrived and that is gathering speed and power is saying that denial will no longer be tolerated. You all must take responsibility for what you do. You've been given the great gift of choice, and you are here to learn how to use it. It really is just that simple.

Forgiveness is *always* held back by blame. When you blame, in essence what you are saying is that you have the right to judge whether a person or group of people is right or wrong according to *you*.

> When you decide that someone is wrong—
> even if it's you deciding you yourself are
> wrong—all of a sudden, you become certain.
> You have cut off curiosity. You are no
> longer open. You are closed. You have made
> a decision. *Wrong*. You have made a
> *judgment*. It is wise to know the difference.

People have believed for a long time, that if they forgave someone, they were letting them off the hook. When you forgive, it doesn't mean you're saying that it's okay that a person went out and murdered someone, or that you agreed with the action. What you're saying is that you *don't know*. They're not right. They're not wrong. You don't know. You don't know what happened in that situation. You don't know if karma was being repaid. You don't know if there was a deep service happening.

A few years ago, a man went into an Amish schoolhouse and held children prisoners, killed them, and then killed himself. Everyone was outraged, because the service these children provided was not understood. The family of the man who murdered the children and then took his own life were invited to the funeral because the Amish wanted to show love to them, to say, *"We forgive, we understand and we forgive, as a group, as a people."*

Now, these are powerful services that people sign up for. These children chose that experience for what it would bring to the collective, which was an enormous gift and has had great impact. *You don't know what you cannot know.* You don't know about the contracts and the millions of events that had to take place, one moment at a time, to bring all these people together to create this one act. You don't know. And saying that you *do* know is a disservice to both you *and* the collective. You are not honoring yourself by being certain.

You can *feel* a knowing that is right for you—you can get intuitive understanding about others—but you will never deeply know what is right or wrong for anyone else, no matter what is happening or what has been done. When you stop blaming others, forgiveness rushes in to fill the void. It's extraordinary. In some ways, you don't have to forgive. Forgiveness is what naturally occurs when you surrender the blame.

This is what happens with blame—and for those of you that have had a less than idyllic childhood, you have watched this progression—you start out blaming your parents, or your family for what happened to you or for who you are, and then you tend to keep adding to the blame over time. It gets bigger and bigger and bigger, and all of a sudden, you are forty years old and you've never taken responsibility for your life, because it's *all their fault* anyway! If they hadn't done *X*, you wouldn't be *Y*!

Blame never, ever, just stays in a nice tidy little box or corner. It always grows. And you always feed it, because it must be fed. It is an energy that is ultimately based in darkness. Darkness must be fed to grow and to survive. It's always looking for more people to blame. *This person does that just like my mother used to, let's blame her! (And him, and them, and those people over there...)*

You will find that blame is running just below the surface in much of your life—blame for the economy, war, murder, hunger; all the things that you feel should be different that fill you with blame.

When you feel that anything that is or was,
should not have been or should not be now,
then you are casting blame on someone or
something. Here's the really difficult part

for people to understand; because we are all
one, every single time you blame another,
you blame yourself. You can never escape
the collective—you *are* the collective—there
is no *them* and *us*, there is only *we*. For a
short time you will be an *I*, but that *I* is
always part of the *we*. You cannot be
separate.

What tends to happen when blame runs like an underground stream through your life is that the person you end up blaming the most is yourself. Then your issues around feeling not good enough crop up—not smart enough, not well enough, not rich enough, not funny enough, not pretty enough—all the *not enough* come from blame. What you are *really* saying is that you are not as you think you *should* be.

Enlightenment is not about learning at all. You're already enlightened, right now, as you sit and read this. Enlightenment is simply the process of knowing it. That's all. The key to getting out of the box you're in is utterly simple. The door's been standing open the whole time; you just didn't notice. You don't have to learn all of this. You already know it. It's a part of you. It's not even buried—it's right in front of you—it's simply been waiting for you to notice.

How do you feel when you blame someone? Does it feel great? If it doesn't, don't do it. When you love someone, when you forgive someone, when forgiveness rushes in, that feels great, truly great. Your heart is light. A smile's on your face. You feel ten years, twenty, thirty, fifty years younger, because all of a sudden you've simply chosen to stop blaming. The burden that you and the collective have been carrying around all these years is gone.

Ceasing to blame someone for something,
does not mean that you now magically
should think what was done was a loving
choice. Learn to just look at your feelings
about the things that happen to you and
your friends, or that you read about in the
media. You can feel the dark energy around
that, you can feel the pain of it, but to move
from your feelings into blame is a choice.
To make someone wrong for what they did,
or right for what they did, is a decision *you*
make. What they did may seem terrible
and make you feel sick, but be careful about
stepping into the judgment of *I know*.

One of the reasons you blame and judge is because you
don't want to sit with the feelings. If something is awful and
feels terrible to you, you make a judgment. *Murderer!
Terrible! Wrong! Put him in jail!* Then after a time you forget
about it, and think now you can go on. But what if you were
to recognize that it's perfectly wonderful and acceptable to
sit and look at whatever it is you're feeling, and just let
yourself *feel* it? Learn to let go of those feelings, and
recognize that it's perfectly all right to feel something
without *doing* anything with the feeling. You don't have to
do anything with your experience at all. You can just let
yourself have it.

When you want to be right, when you are
blaming, even over the smallest thing, stop
for a moment, take a deep breath and say,
*"Okay, Mother said that I might have feelings
that I try to cover up by making judgments.*

*So, I'm going to take a deep breath, and just
sit for a minute to check in with myself."*
And then ask yourself,
*"What am I really feeling about this?
What's happening for me?"*

Judgment seems like the easier way, but the price you pay for it literally goes on for lifetimes. *Literally*. It's not just Hitler that has things to work through, or not just really, really, *bad* people, either—it's *all* of you. The unrest in the world, the war and crime, all of you have to work through that together. Every time you choose to don a body, you choose to be a part of the human collective and everything that goes on within it.

If you start, just with yourself, of letting go of your practice of judgment, the need to be right about strangers, friends, and family, won't matter anymore. When you can let that go, then you (and here's the really great part, you ready?) no longer have to carry the burden of the collective. That's your door prize, because it's no longer a burden energetically. You begin to understand the finer points, the subtitles of darkness and light, and what is truly the essence of love.

Forgiveness is an art, and an art that must be practiced daily, because blame is about separation. Believing that the people *over there* that do *bad* things don't belong to you, and that you can kill them or lock them away for the safety of society, is really for your comfort and denial. It keeps you from having to face yourselves as a collective; so that you don't have to face the deeper meaning. It's why your government wages a war on drugs, rather than facing the needs of drug users within its own sphere of influence and helping them heal. It's so much easier to declare war on *other* people who are growing poppies in some *other* country, than it is to focus on the thousands and thousands who are in your collective, in your own country, right here, right now.

There are some that do focus on that aspect, and, of course, they are the ones that you all look at and say, *"Isn't it wonderful what they're doing for no money, long hours, and very little thanks?"*

You can wonder what kind of karma they may be working through, and how they are helping the collective stay solid and unified.

Each of you is growing exponentially on your spiritual journey. You are feeling and discovering new things about yourself quickly. The way you look at life is shifting almost daily. Your judgment must be included in your awareness. What I recommend is that you do some writing about this if you have not already done so.

Write about anything, anyone, or any group that you blame. Maybe you still blame the Spaniards for the Inquisition... who knows? Write about all the things that you feel you are *right* about concerning relationships, politics, society, and religion. Once you have them all written down, ask yourself,
"Do I really know this for sure? Can I be one hundred percent positive about this judgment?" Go through each judgment and ask, *"Do I keep this one or can I let it go?"* Being one hundred percent positive in your answer, means that you must be one hundred percent positive about everyone and anything involved. If you discover that

*you do feel that way, then keep that
judgment; it's a good one. If, however, after
some consideration you decide you're only
ninety-nine percent sure that you're right,
then I highly recommend you think about
letting that one go.*

Needing to know, needing to be right, needing old beliefs and structures to stay unexamined, are all things that keep old paradigms safe. But they are only old paradigms for those of you on a spiritual path, not for everyone in the world. Lots of people still very much need that paradigm to feel any sort of safety; they need to know that their life has a beginning, middle, and end, and what it's most likely to look like in-between.

You are deconstructing the walls and are asking for freedom of Spirit, freedom of mind, freedom of heart, and freedom of body. If, indeed, you truly want this, then you must be responsible for it. If you don't want to play by the established rules, then you have to make your own. You have to pay attention. You have to make *discernments*—not *judgments*. Your life has to have some kind of structure so that you can live in harmony with the world around you, instead of at odds. Freedom is not anarchy. Freedom is harmony.

Sometimes the beginning of freedom looks like chaos—it can also feel like chaos—but ultimately, you are moving towards harmony. You will be much more interested in being happy and serene, than right. I hope that you never again believe that your judgments about people, groups, or institutions that you don't know and that you are not involved with, have no impact.

Even if you are standing around the food table at a party talking about particular judgments you hold about how your country is being run (or not being run, depending on your view), please understand that your words, your beliefs, and your blame have impact. Most powerfully, they impact *you*—when you blame you add to the burden, then that burden must be balanced again—and guess who has to balance it? *You*, who is a part of the *whole*; there is no *them*; there is only *us*.

You are each responsible for everything you do. This is not to make you feel crazy. You don't have to be hyper-aware and vigilant all the time. That's not what it's about at all. You may console yourself by knowing that you probably have a few more lifetimes to work a lot of this out. You never go backwards. What you obtain in this life, the consciousness you gain, carries on into your next life. You won't have to start at square one. Every progression lasts the entire existence of you as an individual.

Judgments arise when you don't want to feel. Discernment is based on feeling. Discernment is about you, the individual. You can discern that this person over here is not someone you wish to spend time with; you don't need to try and figure out why; it doesn't matter why. You trust yourself. You trust this soul that is more and more prominent every day in your life. You trust it.

For instance, if you meet someone that you don't like very much, your old Self may say that you should like her, that she's just fine and never did anything to you. And then the lecture begins; don't give in to it. Your soul has discerned that no, this is not a good friendship; this is not a good match for you. It doesn't matter why; it doesn't have to be because one of you is wrong and one right or that one of you is good and one bad. It has nothing to do with any of that. It has to do with your Soul saying, "Please, do not get close to that person! They're not right for you at this time in your life!" Maybe you're struggling with an issue that you can't get out from under, and this person has the same issue times ten. The two of you together would drown in self-pity. You're just two people trying to get through your issues, and you can't help each other right now.

Your soul does not judge. Your soul tells you not to be in relationship with this person because you aren't good for each other. Your soul feels the same love for them as it does for a best friend, but it knows what is best for you. That is discernment.

There is an adorable little saying in your culture that suggests that when you point one finger at someone else, you'll soon have three pointing back at you. Cliché, yes; but true. I encourage you to remember it, because who hasn't committed a murder or two in their mind? Who hasn't wished bad things to happen, sometimes to very good people? Who hasn't imagined doing awful things to other people, even if they don't act it out in real life? The deeper you go into this life, the more you realize that the physical is only one aspect of who you really are—an important one—but only one. If you place all of your vision and judgment on the physical, you will tend to see things as very black or white.

> For your own growth and enlightenment,
> for your own blossoming, stay curious.
> When you think you know something
> about someone else, stop and ask yourself,
> "Do I? Do I really know what he or she
> should or should not be doing?"

Another thing I'd like to suggest is that you watch your side comments, please. The comments that you like to imagine you're just tossing out there casually, are generally where most of your poison is placed. There's a way you humans have of assigning blame. As you become more enlightened, more conscious, and more spiritual, you may discover a thought roaming around in your head that says, "Well, maybe I shouldn't really be saying these kinds of things anymore." But there's also something else inside of you that just really wants to say it. You may think no one notices these little off-handed comments that you're tossing out there—but what you're actually doing is throwing poison at the collective, as well as the person you said it too. You are poisoning the well. I ask you to pay attention to that, because the well of the collective on this planet is getting more toxic every day.

> When you let go of judgment and blame,
> you make room for your own experience.
> You create the space to ask yourself, "What
> am I really feeling? What am I experiencing
> as a result?" There will also be more room
> for you to explore the answers to, "What
> can I do? What can I bring to this? How can
> I serve?" That is when the energy of
> forgiveness becomes huge, and fills your
> life.
> When you can abstain from judgment and
> placing blame, you give yourself room to
> become aware of whatever feeling and
> experience you're *really* having; then you
> can ask, *"How can I serve?"* from a place of
> peace. You read about a murderer, and you
> ask, *"How can I serve?"* Maybe the answer
> is to hold *all* the people involved in light,
> love, and kindness. Hold them all in the

energy of the forgiveness you are now
feeling; give it away.

What comes to you from God, you give it away. You feel it, and you give it away, because the collective is starving for forgiveness—*starving* for it. But now *you* know there is an endless supply. Every time you are willing to suspend judgment, every time you are willing to let go of the blame that you carry, a little bit at a time, little bit more, little bit more—until suddenly there is more forgiveness available to you, so more that you can give to others.

You have become creative in how you blame and formulate your judgments, which is why the art of forgiveness requires you to become even more creative, to understand where it's missing in your life, to see the people of your past just as they were, or as they are—fallible human beings—full of difficulties, issues, and problems. Does it make what they did to you any less painful? It will when you feel forgiveness. That is the great joy of it.

When you finally stop judging and blaming your past for its burdens, the forgiveness that comes from finally letting it go will take away the pain you've been carrying around. The pain won't go until you stop the judgment and blaming; plain and simple.

> The best way to let go of your judgments is
> to write them down. Look at them. Feel
> them. Get deep into your feelings and ask,
> "What is here for me? Please, Mother, reveal
> to me what I need to understand so that I
> may serve."

Forgiveness is the ultimate kindness you can do for yourself and others. When you stop blaming and judging yourself, there's little pain in life. Once you set down that burden, only lightness is left; a buoyancy that carries you, nurtures you, encourages you, supports you, and loves you.

> *As you write down your judgments and sit with them, keep asking yourself, "Does this make me feel safe anymore? Is this something that I still need to hang on to?" If the answer is, "Yes," then trust that, and keep moving through it. Know that you're not going to let go of all of it at once. It's going to take some time—as it should.*

The more time that you spend letting go of these behaviors, the easier and less painful your life will become. I promise, I promise, I promise. Let forgiveness become a way of life for you; not something you *have* to do. Don't think, *Well, I'm in pain, so I guess I'll try to forgive so I can feel better.* Look at forgiveness as a new way of life, because ultimately, in the end, you are the one that carries the most pain when you hang on to blame anyway. Not the person who did whatever they did to you. They have their own pain, or maybe not. Maybe they don't think about what they did at all, even though you think about it every day.

> *If you're stubbornly holding on to something, ask yourself, "Is this still worth hanging on to? Who is this hurting the most?" Generally, the answer will be you.*

Love yourself enough to explore forgiveness. Have the courage to look at your judgments and blame as honestly and with as much love and kindness as you possibly can.

Make the commitment to yourself that you will not participate in judgment or blame any longer, to the very best of your ability. Ask to be shown when you are participating in it, so that you can make the shift. The best thing that comes with forgiveness is heightened consciousness—*leaps* forward in consciousness—energetic ability, communion, real connection with the people in your life, intimacy.

If you have a mountain of blame and judgment between you and another person, know that you're going to carry that mountain with you wherever you go. It's always going to be between everyone and you. It makes communion hard. You have to tunnel beneath that mountain and dynamite blast your way through it. When you finally let it go, when you stop practicing judgment and blame, all of a sudden you'll have the freedom to genuinely commune. It's easy to connect; not only with other people, but also with the Divine. You won't feel so cut off.

Don't forget to include God (and me!) on your list. You may sometimes think we're not getting it right, or that our timing is wrong, or that if we'd only step in and do this or that, there would be no more war, no famine, no torture. But if you will look at these things in and of themselves for what they really are, you'll realize that you're not changing the world by sitting in judgment, you're not ending hunger by blaming us because there is hunger. As a matter of fact, you hold yourself back from finding the solution when you blame.

If you truly want to be of service, if you want to give your life to God, then you have to let go of the idea that you know better than God! The irony is that when you let go of trying to play God, you'll find your own God-self. Your Divinity will shine through, because God and I don't have judgment. The more judgment you have, the more mired in the darker aspects you become. Your Divinity lies in forgiveness. Your God-self knows this. I am asking for your human-self to just notice, that's all. Just notice.

MEDITATION:

Sit quietly and close your eyes. Take a nice deep breath. Good. Now I'd like for you to breathe in and out of your heart chakra. With each breath, I'd like you to feel it opening more and more. As you breathe in and out of your heart, and as you feel it expand, I'd like for you just to notice how this expansion feels, how this heart center really feels as you open. I want more than anything for you to just feel the simplicity of breathing in and out from your heart, and how this gives you space to just be with your own experience; how this practice gives you permission to feel whatever it is that you are feeling right now, in this moment. Your heart knows how to make room for you. When you feel the need, breathe in and out through your heart, and allow it to make room for you to have your experience without judgment; without blame. Something as simple as breathing in and out of your heart gives you permission to just feel. Wonderful. Take three deep breaths and let go of the meditation. You may open your eyes.

Always remember, with this and everything else, ask for help, ask for help, ask for help, ask for help. You shall receive it.

I thank you for allowing me to serve you on this evening. It is always my great joy to do so.

Namaste ~

CHAPTER 10
Blame, Inc.

I have heard it said by Mother and many other extraordinary beings, both embodied and not, that forgiveness is the key to happiness. I have experienced its healing magic throughout my life. Why then, is it still so hard to do, when I know it is the answer to a particular problem?

I lost faith in life after my parent's divorce, the death of my father, grandmother, dog, and my mother's remarriage, all of which occurred within two years. At thirteen, I didn't consciously blame anyone for those losses, but it was there, hiding in the shadows. Blame filled the holes left behind by the ones who were gone, and I can now see and feel the tendrils of poison that it wove into everything. Before that time, like most children, I blamed and forgave with equal swiftness. At the end of those two years, it was as if my forgiveness switch had broken. It wasn't that I didn't *want* to forgive; I had just forgotten how, and that it felt good to do so.

As a child, I instinctively knew forgiveness lightened my soul. Because love existed inside of me, blame was unable to take root until I lost those I loved. People told me I would always have my loved ones in my heart, but I thought that was a poor substitute for living, breathing individuals. I had never been an angry person, so was at a loss when the feeling of rage rose up inside of me and clawed to get out. Too afraid to give it a voice, I became its gatekeeper.

The price I paid for repressing my anger, born of fear, was to become a person of blame. Resentment festered. I lost my confidence and collapsed in on myself. Blame is the righteous costume for resentment and fear. Blame disguised itself in the fantasy of being a wise Solomon, judging everyone around me. If I decided others were wrong, I got to feel superior; and if someone was right, I became lower than a Nevada lake during a drought and unworthy of even simple kindness. I never felt equal.

This hidden process took my child-self from having wide-eyed connection to nature and being able to feel life pulsing in me and all around me, to feeling as though I were living in a fun house with my young adult-self stuck in front of its mirrors, cringing at the distorted images. I was unable to discern where I belonged.

My resentment flared up with the least provocation. I blamed others for my misfortunes. Both feelings coated my perception of the world, and turned bright colors to ash. My constant judgment of myself and the people I loved and cared about created an ever widening gap between us. It felt like the Grand Canyon—too big to jump and with seemingly no way to go around.

My dream of a creative, fulfilling life remained just that—a dream. My fears fed my resentments which fed my judgment and blame. I was either sitting atop my defensive walls looking down on others, or cowering behind them, hiding in shame. None of that left room for exploration, discovery, or achievement.

Mother speaks of forgiveness coming as the result of letting go of blame. Sounds great, but the actual internal process is, and I suspect always will be, a mystery to me. I have stopped trying to define this mystery because it interrupts the process of letting go for me. The mystery of my inner life moves me into my feelings and out of my thoughts. It is my feelings, and not necessarily my emotions, that lead me to discover myself.

The first thing that I had to do was become aware of my blame. I honestly didn't know it existed. From the beginning of my spiritual life at twenty-seven, and still now, the most powerful prayer for me is, *Thy will not mine be done.* My will had me abusing drugs, alcohol, and binging on food every day. So when someone suggested this simple prayer to me, I thought, *Good God, yes, anyone's will but mine—because mine is killing me.*

I spoke this prayer on my knees every morning and all throughout the day. It gave me a sense of comfort, then and now. Life began to feel like a co-creation between the Divine and myself. I had my part to do, and Spirit had Hers. No matter how much I wanted to be in charge of Spirit's part, I couldn't be. Awakening to my own part, accepting it and loving it, became my vocation. Awakening to the degree of blame I had been creating, and continued to create, was staggering. It knocked me off my feet for days at a time. Peeking through the curtain into my shadow was not something I could do on my own. It was empowering to know that I didn't have to look at any of it alone.

I was incapable of exploring my shadow by myself. I'm not the type of person to walk down a dark alley without a big, burly angel by my side. I avoid the alley or find a safer, less revealing route. If I'm going to dive in, I have to know that I'm as safe as I can be. Even though Mother Mary had not yet come to me when I first began to awaken, She sent an angel first to prepare the way. She knew I wouldn't budge unless I felt the presence of something that could protect me from the dark.

When the revelation of Self began, there were days when the only thing I could manage was to get up off the couch and go to work, dragging myself through the day. It went in cycles. I had enough energy most days to function normally. Other days I was wiped out. My new relationship with the Divine bolstered my micro-confidence enough to discover that I was not without courage, as I had come to believe. The ingrained habit of becoming overwhelmed and then collapsing was beginning to change. Who would I be without that pain cycle? My mind couldn't see that far ahead, but my heart could. Spirit breathed life and volume into my heart. I could hear my still, small voice and feel wonder again.

I don't know why, but amnesia has been an active part of my spiritual growth. There are days when I am wrestling with a problem that feels like an anaconda wrapped around me, choking my life force, as I valiantly try to subjugate this giant snake to my will. As I drag it along with me, asking friends what I should do, they in turn ask me with perfect sincerity, "Have you asked Mother? Have you prayed about it?"

Well, damn. No, I haven't. I look the snake in the eye and see sympathy for my ongoing density. It is nodding its head in agreement with my friends, knowing it can be unwound from my neck and dispatched with help from Mother and my inner Spirit.

In Mother's brilliance, She encourages me to face my blame and assures me that forgiveness will flow naturally as a result of that surrender. My amnesia lets me hang onto my blame, because as soon as I pray, I feel Divine love. But if I'm willing to break off the smallest chunk of my wall and hand it over to Mother, love fills the gap, which inspires me to let go of a little more until the need for forgiveness begins to outweigh my habit of blame.

Forgiveness has grown within me, and now, after twenty-two years, it has become more the habit. Blame is less a part of my daily life. Even as I write this, I feel the old blame pointing its finger and looking down at me from on high and saying, "Twenty-two years!? Obviously, you are hopeless!" The greater light within answers, *"Love does not know time. Feel the love within you; that is what matters the most."*

Mother Mary still gets the brunt of my blame. I feel completely free to blame Her for everything and dump it all in Her enormous, capable hands. She loves me, and all of us, unconditionally. When I direct my blame at Her, I know there is a much greater chance She will show me what to do with it while She helps me carry it.

I still occasionally get stuck in believing that if I let my blame go, the other person will get off without a penalty. More importantly, they will not suffer as I am suffering. I really didn't understand the saying *misery loves company* until I began understanding my blame. I wanted everyone to see the extent of my pain, so that they would know firsthand what *their* cruelty felt like when it was directed at *me*. They would get what *I* believed they deserved. This attitude always leads me back to my self-pity-God-complex-martyred-wounded girl.

Mother guides me to wrap my wounds with love, understanding, and for me, humor. My exploration of blame has led me to a few conclusions about myself. Even on my best days I can see life in the distorted fun house mirror. Drama, thy name is Danielle. If I can't find the humor, I get pulled under. I also have the tendency to take life and myself too seriously. Humor is my silver lining. I always stay open to it. It is the one thing sure to bring my experiences into balance.

Not everything is that simplistic, but a shocking amount is. Blame and self-pity give me a bloated sense of my own self-importance. To be able to laugh at myself, not with derision, but with love, is a big part of my surrender of blame.

Understanding is the next key to forgiveness. Of course

I feel the way I do. There's nothing wrong with any of my feelings. They are an experience—nothing more and nothing less. When I remember this, I can love what is happening inside me—I can feel what matters to me—and blame isn't it. When I am able to allow forgiveness in, my whole perspective shifts. I have no desire to carry the burden of blame, and so cast it off easily. I become filled with the knowing that it's not my place to make others pay for their actions. My choice is to decide what I need to do in relation to them, so I can feel safe, loved, cared for, and strong. The rest is up to Spirit, and I gladly hand over the imaginary reins of control.

The relief that follows lets me know that I've done the right thing. Forgiveness fills my heart and soul with kindness and faith, the two things I need to navigate my life with confidence and love.

Sometimes I can only surrender a small piece of the blame I'm holding onto. Other times I can let go of it all. It's the old, unresolved experiences that have grown larger the longer I carry them that need to dissolve in pieces.

Kindness is the aspect of love that works best with my blame. It's not something I excel at when I try to direct it at myself. I often feel like the man who finds himself in the presence of a weeping stranger and is at a loss as to what to do. My inner pats on the back and attempts at soothing noises ring a false tone. I would rather be involved in any distraction rather than comfort myself with kindness. This comes from years of being hard on myself and having unreasonable expectations. I can take a bath, call a friend, get a pedicure, say a prayer— all of these are kind, independent actions—but being kind to my inner self in the moment I'm hurting is still a work in progress. I am getting better at it. Sometimes I forget to sit with myself and say, *"It's going to be okay. You are going to be okay."*

Every moment spent in Mother's presence grants me the experience of forgiveness. Without a word spoken or a teaching given, I am bathed in redemption of Self. Her grace reveals my glory, both shadow and light, and at the end of the day, I feel it's okay to be me. So I've decided to stay close to Her, because when I have to walk down the dark alley of blame, it is Mother I want by my side.

CHAPTER 11
Illusion of separation

As you read these words, they will integrate into your heart, softening it so that you will be able to receive more of my gifts to you, which are held within these teachings. Already you are allowing a more spacious existence, and we are only half way through. Wonderful! Now I will help you to remove one of the primary energies that you hold within— the illusion of separation, which keeps you from being in relationship with yourself. Separation is a subject that is often thought about in your culture. You yearn for union, and yet often feel separate in your existence, in your lives with each other, and with the Divine. Often, what I feel from you is loneliness. You sometimes speak of this to friends and loved ones—that you are lonely, feeling isolated, adrift. I'd like to shift your perspective on this perception.

Even though you might feel that the spiritual goal for your human life is to find union—Divine union—I'd encourage you to let go of that goal. If for no other reason, so that it doesn't continue to make you crazy trying to reach it. The union is already there, within you. It's not something that you have to chase. I like to think of it more as just getting out of your own way.

Part of your evolution as a spiritual being, is the simple awakening to the experience of union that already exists—not only within you, but also for you in relation to the world.

Your beginnings in the human cycle of evolution contain a vast feeling of separation. It's interesting that in the beginning, you didn't care about that separation because you were too busy living your human life. As you have evolved—birth, death, and re-birth, in different bodies, different times, and different places—there is an awakening process that takes place within you. An awakening that says, *"I think there's something more than just this human existence, this flesh, this work out in the world, other humans. I feel something greater, something bigger."* Then, the trouble starts.

You start yearning for something beyond, something greater than yourself, for a communion that, when touched, is more glorious than anything you've ever experienced. Some people only need touch it once to want to leave behind the everyday human world and concentrate on only that feeling for the rest of their lives.

As you cycle through your lives and evolve, you start to divide your perception between the human and the Divine. At a certain point (and this lifetime might be that point for most of you), there will be a great and deep frustration with the human aspect of your life and world, and a longing for communion. This can sometimes seem to create more frustration than it alleviates. You want to know why you can't take that feeling out into the world, your job, to the people that are shouting at you to hurry up, slow down, do this, do that. Your impatience with your spouse, your children, and the world makes you wonder if you're doing your right work; if you're on the right path.

The spiritual life becomes the heart of you. It's what you need more than anything else in order to find fulfillment. So you try to reconcile that feeling of expansiveness, depth, and beauty with what is around you in the world. There are days when it's easier and days when it's harder. You begin to struggle with the question of being separate.

Your world is evolving collectively at a very powerful rate. Your population is exploding. Even though there are more people, there is less community. More people live isolated, singular, insular lives. It feels like a disconnection. But even if you're not living in that manner, you are still a part of the collective, and being a part of the collective affects your consciousness. Sometimes you may not even be feeling your own loneliness, but rather that of the collective's sense of isolation.

When people come together in community, there is revelation. It's harder to hide in a community; there are people who care about you and are focused on you, who really want to know how you are, and who accept you as you are. Sometimes that's not easy to find, and sometimes, when you have it, you don't want it. Believe me when I tell you that I understand intimately the problems that you deal with day to day in the human world. I hear and feel it *all*.

Your isolation as a collective is part of the evolution of the One, or the mass human experience. You are realizing more and more profoundly, what community once gave you. When mankind was young, everyone had to live together in order to survive. You took things for granted because that was just how it was. You didn't know another way. But since, you've been given the opportunity to live separate, more isolated lives—it has been an extraordinary experiment—but now you're coming back around to understanding the old saying, "United we stand, divided we fall."

You have discovered tools that will help bring things back around for you to have a very different experience, an experience that is based in community; but this time not so much for survival, but by *choice*.

Isolation keeps you from the inner experience of Self. To isolate in your modern world requires a lot of electronic devices, a lot of chatter, and a lot of chaos. You can be very successful doing this, but the price you pay is rather high. It costs you your serenity, your sense of peace within, which is what provides you the ability to feel as One.

If you were to visit a monastery, an ashram, a church, and other types of gatherings where those that attend are focused on Spirit, on God, one of the things you might notice that they have in common is the quiet. There's no loud music, car horns, yelling or chatter. People who feel drawn to commune with Spirit tend to seek out silence, quiet. There is a reason for that. As humans, you are very much in the physical world. The physical world affects you deeply, as it should, because you are here to experience it, to revel in it, to enjoy it, to explore it.

> *If you find yourself desiring more union,*
> *then you must also seek silence. I don't*
> *necessarily mean just through meditation.*
> *Although I encourage everyone to have a*
> *daily meditation practice, it is the quiet*
> *that resides within you always that I am*
> *speaking of now.*

The illusion of separation comes when you believe that what you need in life is outside of you; that what you seek the answer to in relation to your problems, issues, fears, or worries is outside of you. As a human, it makes complete sense that you would feel this way. It's difficult to shift one's perception from believing that the outward changes the inward, rather than the other way around. If you could just meet your soul mate, you would be happy. If you could find your right work in life, your purpose, you would be happy.

If you could make enough money so that you wouldn't worry so much about the bills, you could be happy... These thoughts and ideas are a continuation of the belief that those things will generate the peace and happiness that you desire, rather than knowing that they already reside within you.

It's easy to listen to someone like me say that, but it's something else entirely to believe it. Yes, you want to know, *Where, exactly, are they within? Are they written on tablets embedded in one of my organs that I could just take out and study? Where are they written? How can I read them? How can I access them? I have an appointment in an hour and I need to know now. There is so much happening around me that I have to be a part of while I'm trying to figure out these other things within.*

I can honestly tell you that you walk a difficult path in this life. You are not faint of heart. You are almost straddling two worlds; the human and the spiritual. Your goal in this life is to merge the two. I want to bring you closer to the understanding and the experiential knowing that you are not separate from yourself, or anyone else.

The reality is that your bodies are separate. You inhabit your body. You are not joined at the skin; you are detached from others. You have your life, which you go about living, and they have theirs; your lives are different. Yes, of course, there is separation. You don't want their lives, and they don't want yours. You might want elements of someone else's life. You may think they have a great thing going on, so you want that and that and that thing they have to add to your own life. But in truth, you would never want to go and actually inhabit someone else's life. For better or worse, even though you might not feel it sometimes, you really do want your own life, because it belongs to you. It is yours.

You have chosen a level of ownership in this life that is

very powerful, and you don't give it up lightly. Most of you fight for it tooth and nail, even while you complain about that very life. The tenacity of human beings is extraordinary, glorious, because you come again and again and again to say, *"I'm willing. I'm willing. I'm here, and I'm willing."*

You are living your own life and that is as it should be. Let go of the belief that you should somehow be living the same life as someone else. Being part of the One does not mean that you give up your life in order to live the same life that everyone else is living. Trust me when I tell you that we really do not want to create just one kind of human. You are all individuals, and you're glorious in your individuality; your unique way of doing things, of looking at life—your unique laughter, your smile, your tears—all extraordinary. No, you wouldn't want to be someone else, to be the same as someone else, to give up your individuality; no.

When I speak of the *One*, I mean to say that there is no separation within your Self. Stop fighting yourself. Stop keeping yourself separate from your Self. I call this holding yourself back or repressing yourself. When you let yourself go, if you get out of the way, *that* is the One. When you feel whole and One within yourself (which is the byproduct of that wholeness), then you will feel the connection with everyone and everything around you. But now you will do it in a way that allows you to be connected, but not merged into one flesh, one being. You retain that which is unique and wonderful unto you. Yet, you get to share that uniqueness, and also experience other's uniqueness, because you're not trying to prove that your way of living is the only acceptable way of living.

Be careful of all the teachings that are swirling around. Be careful that what you say you believe in, is what you actually believe in, because in the fervor of spiritual teaching, often, what is forgotten, is *you*. You are here in this life to find union with yourself, and that's not to be found out there. It's within; always within. When the union with yourself becomes deeper and deeper, you cannot help but be in union with God, because you *are* God. Where else would you come from? What else would you be made of? Your atoms, your molecules, everything—it's all just creation, just energy vibrating, and at a certain level it creates your body, and everyone else's body. Surely, you learned this in science, in high school.

You know what you are. You are energy, pure energy. This is the creation of God, of Spirit. (What you call it doesn't matter.) It just is. So, where do you go when what you are seeking, in the end, is all One? You are given this precious life, this body, this mind, this heart, so that you can discover yourself as Divine; not in spite of being human, but *because* you're human.

> The union you seek is with yourself. Where do you fight yourself? Where do you hold yourself back? Where do you keep saying to yourself, "Maybe tomorrow; right now I'm too tired... I'll wait... Oh, well, *she* can do that, but *I* could never do that... Why does *he* have that, when *I* don't?"

Each one of you has this internal struggle, and at this point in your evolution, I guarantee that you are spending more energy holding yourself back, than just letting go. It's why so many of you struggle with fatigue and other vague health issues, when the doctors say that they can't really find anything in particular wrong. So then you go to a natural practitioner, and they tell you that your chi is low, and your adrenals are in terrible shape, and you need to take this herb, and do that exercise, and *still* you're tired. It's because you're expending enormous amounts of energy holding on to that which, inherently, just wants to relax and let go.

Try not to put things into categories. For example, let's say you've always wanted to be a painter and are holding yourself back from painting. Don't decide that you know what you're holding yourself back from, because then you'll get a hundred steps ahead and miss the energy of holding yourself back. You'll bypass it, because you're too busy analyzing it. Just *trust*. Sit with the feeling inside you. Try not to put a name on it. Instead, just notice if the energy feels heavy, repressive, as if you can't quite move through it.

For many of you in this life, the practice of holding yourself back has been terribly important; a point of survival for some of you. Try not to look at this as the enemy, but as your *friend*. You cannot feel it all at once. You cannot instantly be in union with yourself and have everything revealed. You would literally not survive the experience.

It must be a gradual movement.

My gift to you, is to take away that next thing, that next piece of energy that holds you back—but here's my disclaimer—taking that away may feel too frightening to you. If so, I will give it back to you, but we might

> have a bit of a tug of war, because I'm going
> to try to convince you to let me keep it. In
> the end, if you insist, I will, however, give it
> back.

I do ask that you make the attempt to go within, to change your perception about union, about separation, and to understand that it's yourself that you really seek to have union with. And I don't mean in a selfish way, such as thinking you're all that you need, and you don't need any one else. Just see what happens when you are more in union with yourself. When you stop fighting yourself to such extremes, the outside takes care of itself; career, purpose, jobs, relationships, money, homes, cars, families. Surprisingly enough, that's *not* the battleground.

> I'm suggesting that you decide, from this
> day forward, not to show up for the war
> anymore. Decide that you're not going to
> fight yourself, and that you're going to say
> yes to yourself. Because you are each
> unique, it's going to feel different for each
> of you. You have to go within and first
> discover what it feels like when you say *no*
> to yourself. What is the actual feeling
> inside when you say *no*, when you battle
> yourself, when you are struggling
> inside? Where do you feel it? What does it
> feel like? Get to know yourself.

Yes, you can change jobs, spouses, careers, homes, and in some ways, you may see vast improvement in your life—more happiness, a better sense of well-being, a calmer outlook—all of these wonderful things. But in the end, union with your own soul is the thing you yearn for more than anything else. All these other things feel good, and you will enjoy them. Sometimes you'll get happiness, sometimes pain. You'll get lost in life and all the things around you, but over and over and over again, you'll come back to the yearning. That yearning feels more important to you, whether you can admit it aloud or not, than children, money, spouses, and jobs; more important than any of it.

There may be a very human part of you that wants all these wonderful things in life, and you want to be able to say, "Look what I've done! I've fixed my insides to such an extent, that I'm attracting lots of good stuff into my life!" But it's never enough, it's just not the *right* thing; not for you. For you, it's only the union that really matters, because when you feel it, that's it—that's *the* feeling—it's your completion.

> You will have moments of deep communion, and you can call them whatever you like. Whether communing with Mother, God, Spirit, or Self, this is what you yearn for. I am here not only to help you feel union more deeply, but to tell you that you have it within already. The search is over. It's up to you to allow yourself to feel it. Stop fighting yourself, and always feeling you're not doing something right, or that if you could just do it a little better, a little more, or a little faster, then *somehow* your life would *finally* be good. I'd like for you, please, as a great kindness to me, to stop being so hard on

yourselves! Don't always assume that
things are going wrong because there's
something you're not doing. This feeling of
separation comes from something you *are*
doing, and that is fighting yourself. I would
request a little less *doing* from you, rather
than *more*.

It's not as if I'm asking you to be satisfied with just a robe, sandals, and a begging bowl. That's not necessary either. I'm not asking you to give up your dreams, your aspirations, or anything about your outer life that you feel is important to you. On the contrary, I ask you to embrace it, to revel in it. It is your life, after all. There's so much in it to enjoy, to explore.

I'm asking that you start to shift your
perception. If you shift within, the feeling
of separation, of feeling alone out in the
world or in relation to it, will disappear.

MEDITATION:

Sit quietly and close your eyes. Take three deep breaths. As you breathe, open your hands and place them on top of your thighs, resting comfortably, right hand on right leg; left hand on left leg.

Take three deeper, stronger breaths, in and out through your nose. Awaken your senses, wake up your body. Let go of your thoughts; let them drift in and out.

Find any energy within that feels repressed, that feels held back, or that feels dense or burdensome.

Just sit with these feelings. Don't do anything with

them, just sit with them. Feel them. Become familiar with your own Self.

Feeling yourself, rather than *thinking* about yourself, will lessen the struggle within. Just feel what's there with no expectation. The *reasons* you hold yourself back, don't matter; just be with the feeling of it. You don't have to know why you hold yourself back, or the origins of your repression.

As you feel the density, breathe into it. Find the willingness within to relax your hold on it, just a little bit more with each breath.

Feel the commitment within yourself; don't think it. Feel your commitment to surrendering the battle, without having to know who's won and who's lost. Breathe in my gift to you. Your willingness to receive is all that you need with this breath, in this moment.

Feel the energy of repression as a gift that's been important and necessary to your individual life. You cannot wish it gone, you cannot try to get rid of it, but you can love it. Feel it deeply, and through the feeling of it, allow it to be transformed.

> When you feel what is, you accept.
> When you accept, you can change
> anything.

Now take a deep breath and relax into the possibility of union within your own body, your own mind, your own life. Say a little prayer of thanks for having the wisdom and foresight to receive exactly what you need.

Allow yourself to be grateful for giving yourself such a gift. Go to your knees and place your forehead on the floor, relaxing into child's pose, and grounding your energy into the earth like the roots of a tree. Feel your energy entwining deeply with Mother Earth, allowing her to sustain you, support you, and strengthen you. Slowly sit up, and gently stretch.

I ask you to give away all that you have received here, and know that as you give, I will replenish.

Namaste ~

CHAPTER 12
The hard way or no way

I love Mother's constant acceptance and understanding of what it truly means to be human. When She tells me that something I've been rejecting in myself and classifying as wrong, is perfectly normal and right for me at this point in my evolution, my whole body decompresses and I think, *Thank God*. The stranglehold on me to be what I think I *should* be loosens enough for me to know myself as I *am*.

It sounds simple, and it really is, but it's not easy. This teaching is about acceptance. Mother says that even though we might feel that the goal for us spiritually is Divine union, She encourages us to let go of that goal, so it doesn't drive us crazy trying to reach it. Because let me assure you, I am in that crazy car driving myself into a brick wall. Union is already there, within us. It's not something that we have to set as a goal. That is Her most loving way of saying that I may want to step out of the way and let my life flow.

Now *this* I can get behind! I'm the type who exhausts myself trying to force something to happen. I'm a pusher. In my twenties and early thirties, people used to tell me I was hard on myself. This was not occasional, but consistently said to me, by many people; some who barely knew me. Every time I heard it, I thought, *Really?* I couldn't see it. I would feel annoyed when people said that to me, because I thought I was just trying to reach a goal or get to a certain level of spiritual and emotional enlightenment, and that it simply wouldn't *happen* if I wasn't hard on myself.

The truth is it had to be the hard way for me, or no way. I believed I should suffer for anything good or worth having, including spiritual enlightenment. If I didn't struggle, it wasn't right for me to have it.

The entrance of Mother Mary into my consciousness, my life, changed things. From the first moment She came to me until now, She has felt extraordinary. Our relationship has never been just nice and pleasant, but an overwhelming force that devoured me whole. To me She is the Mother of compassion, and Kali the destroyer, wrapped into one. Kahil Gibran describes my feelings perfectly in his book, *The Prophet*. The chapter on love reads:

Like sheaves of corn he gathers you unto himself. He threshes you to make you naked. He sifts you to free you from your husks. He grinds you to whiteness. He kneads you until you are pliant; and then He assigns you to His sacred fire, that you may become sacred bread for God's sacred feast.

I was terrified. Not because I ever felt for even a moment that Mother would hurt me or lead me down a path that brought misery, but the opposite.

To be devoured by the Divine is to be set free.

When I allow myself to surrender into Her, I feel whole and part of everything. For a long time, I was too desperate to maintain control to allow myself freedom. I deliberately chose the hard way again and again to show Mother that I was the one in charge. I was the one in control of my life. I was not going to give in to Her glory and the wondrous feelings that came with it, because I was terrified of loving it and losing it.

I didn't realize how separated I felt from my life until I experienced my connection with Her. It came easily, and so of course, was immediately suspect. It took me a while to understand the part control played in my illusions of separation. When I try and exert control to manipulate people or situations, I always feel like I'm on my own, that I have to figure it out, make it happen, to ensure that I get what I want. When I don't exert control, I feel like I'm a part of things. It may even feel hard or chaotic, but underneath, there is a knowing that it will come out alright for me. I may not know how or why, I just feel that it will. I sense something greater than myself at work. I am working in conjunction with Mother and the collective, as opposed to being on my own.

I have discovered that I prefer living my life in communion with the Divine, rather than as a lone wolf. I abdicate responsibility less when I allow myself to walk with the Divine, rather than when I get caught up trying to do everything myself. Doing it all on my own shifts me into overwhelm, and I end up doing much less and feeling worn out for my efforts.

It's by my actions and thoughts that I cut myself off from feeling connected to the world, Divine spirit, and myself. People come and go in my life, they live and die, but Mother ensures that I'm never abandoned. There is always room for me at the table, but I have to be the one to claim my seat.

I like being an *I* and having an ego. Mother has shown me that I can be one with Her and maintain my own identity. Now I see this life of mine as a rare gift. No longer do I wish to get rid of my ego, since it defines my perception of Self. I get to laugh at what I find funny, sob over what I find painful, and celebrate my own form of bliss. I can journey with those that feel similar, and at the same time explore diversity. I know I always have a choice, and knowing I have a choice is vital in order for me to feel safe enough to cede control. When I let go enough, I experience union with life.

I still struggle with intimacy, and so am wary of union with others. I can feel the tight hold I maintain on my need to feel separate from everyone around me. That is sometimes the drawback to consciousness, and the union with Self that follows. I can feel my own shadow and all its facets; like an emotional yard sale, everything is on display, to be examined and haggled over just to save a nickel.

Then there are those days when I don't want God to be the answer. *I* want to be the answer. I want everyone and everything to leave me alone. Union with the Divine is scary. I don't want to give up all my possessions and live in a cave on a mountaintop, and spend every day in meditation. I like pedicures and pretty things. I need to skate on the surface sometimes and make an effort to avoid the deep end. I don't have as many of those days as I used to, though. That's how I know I'm moving in the right direction, because I'm less afraid of what's going to happen when I get to where I'm going.

I still worry that Mother will take it all away if I'm not vigilant. She encourages me to run away as often as I need to, and of course, it's this allowance that brings me back to Her. My feral Self craves Her light and love. No matter how much I still fear it, I need it; I yearn for it, and will do anything to have it. So I stay, even when I want to flee. Every moment I am willing to stay, is another moment of love.

CHAPTER 13
A spiritual life

Many of you struggle on your spiritual path—the path you have chosen, and maybe, sometimes, wish that you had not. Many of you stepped onto your spiritual path and embraced it from the beginning, because you felt it would relieve some of the pain and suffering that had come before in your life. Many of you believed it was the solution to your problems, and that it would bring happiness and the life of your dreams. What many of you discovered instead, is that this path brought you into deeper contact with some of your pain, and that it wasn't the cure all that you had hoped for; that it did not, in one broad stroke, relieve you of all of your pain, fears, worries, stress, and anxiety.

For some of you, there is impatience, especially if you've been on the path for a while. When does the fun begin? When is all the pain relieved? When do you have the things in your life that you want and desire and feel that you should have, that others have? You look at them and see all the things you don't have, and they are the very things that *you* want.

Somehow, having a connection to the Divine was supposed to create the fulfillment in your outside life that you wanted—and yet, you're still here anyway, despite not getting what you wanted at different points in your awakening, your enlightenment. I know it's hard to be content with only connection. As a human being, Divine in your own right, you still want your relationships to provide relief from certain stress and worries that you carry with you; relief from those things inside you that still haunt you, and generate pain for you.

A spiritual life is every life.
All life is spiritual.
All life is sacred.
All life is endless.

It doesn't matter what form it takes; a physical life may end, but the Spirit is eternal and evolving, changing, and taking on new forms; some human. What you are really on, is a path of enlightenment. To be enlightened means to be conscious, awake, and aware. You chose this life for a deeply important reason. I know that you want so many good things for yourself and your loved ones. You want relief from your pain—your emotional pain, your fear of loss or not getting what you want, what you feel you need. I want to focus on the deeper meaning of enlightenment, which is the conscious spiritual life you have chosen to embrace and to be a part of.

Your life is important now; *this* physical life. Yes, other lives have been lived—and other lives *will* be lived—but this is your primary life, the most important one. There is so much more to your life in this moment than *just* your physical life, although you're still getting up each day, going to work, trying to create and create and create on the physical level. You are an eternal being, a being of grace and depth the likes of which you are just now discovering. I do not in any way wish to demean your outer, physical life. It's real. It's tangible. It has weight and meaning to you. It is important. But now is about remembering the larger importance of your existence and looking beyond what's in front of you; to move you beyond the limitations of sight, hearing, taste, smell, and touch. They represent only a fraction of what you are capable of feeling.

The path to enlightenment is about sacrifice. What do you sacrifice when you live a life of enlightenment? Sometimes, it's people who don't wish to join you. Sometimes, it's the work you thought you were going to do, in favor of a calling that comes upon you unexpectedly. Sometimes, it's a relationship you once thought would go on forever, but as you changed, they did not. As you awakened, you had less and less in common until there was little left but a sense of caring and kindness between you, but not enough to maintain a friendship, a deep family connection, or an intimate relationship of the romantic type.

> You are asked each day that you walk upon this path to risk losing everything that you hold dear today; your health, your wealth, all the people around you. And yet, what are you given in return for this sacrifice? You are given new work, new friends, new wealth—but only if you are willing to receive it. Whatever falls away from you will be replaced by something different, someone that vibrates and resonates more closely with you, as you are now.

What is it to be enlightened? Enlightenment is to know yourself as God. It is to awaken at every moment to a more expanded feeling, a depth of feeling, a connection that can only be generated from within you, never from the outside. Once it awakens within you, you become aware of that energy pulsating all around you, waiting to connect you to the greatness within the One. Your time here in your chosen body is limited; your Soul, your Spirit is not.

It is important to focus on your physical life, your human life. It is even more important for you to remember each day that you are on a path, a journey of consciousness, and that you chose this path, at this time in your life, to awaken in just such a way as you are awakening right now. You are being granted the gift of moving beyond your immediate senses, of moving beyond your limitations and what you think you know, to enter into a realm of limitless possibility. Not necessarily so you can have more in the physical realm; certain things or a certain someone, but simply to expand and embrace so much more than what many around you are content with.

Trust me when I tell you that you will never just be content with getting all your desires met in the physical world. If you felt you had your soul mate, all the money you felt you required, children, no children, deep close relationships with family, close friends, whatever it is that you desire, if you had it all, you would still look for more. Nothing in the physical will ever, ever fulfill you to the degree that you seek, that you crave.

> When you awaken and begin the conscious
> process of enlightenment, it is not about
> getting certain things in your physical life.
> It's about delving into the depths. This is
> the *more* that you crave, the *more* that calls
> to you.

You are extraordinarily courageous to embark upon a conscious journey because when you wake up, it's a bit like being under anesthesia or taking pain medication; they may dull the pain for a time, but at some point it always wears off. At first, you think the pain is worse than it ever was, because the pain was "gone" and now there it's back. In actuality, the pain never left. You simply became desensitized or anesthetized to the pain; it was just covered up.

So understand that waking up to yourself and the world around you can be painful. You are not creating more pain by choosing this path, however; you are just slowly becoming aware of the pain that always existed. It's not the pain of childhood, nor the pain of not getting what you want, not even the feeling that there is too much loss—though all these things can cause pain—the pain you are *deeply* awakening to, is the pain of *separation*.

In order to become human, in order to be a person, you must be able to identify yourself as *I*. This is what you associate with the ego, but let me say now that the ego is not your enemy, beloved children. It is one of your greatest gifts. To be able to say, "*I Am*," is a singular achievement in creation. It's rare and precious, and should never ever be ignored; never discouraged.

The *I* gives you the ability to be unique; the ability to choose by free will; the ability to have an identity that is separate from others; the ability to explore your gifts, and the things that don't feel like gifts at all, but that only seem to get you into trouble or pain. At the same time, because you are ultimately One with all things—your Spirit is One—your separation, in a sense, is a bit borrowed as you live in a body, perhaps, for a very long time, but it is borrowed.

You know, deeply within yourself, that you are One with all things. While you enjoy your independence on many levels, you enjoy being able to make your own decisions and choices, there is a part of you that longs to no longer feel separate, and to be One again.

What you are embarking on now is a journey to find balance, to be able to feel the Oneness, the connection, while you're still independent and getting to know yourself fully through all your lifetimes and forward. This is a rare gift. It's easy to get caught up in the parts of your life that keep you from recognizing this gift. Some of the pain or loneliness within you is simply due to you awakening to the pain of separation. You are being asked to evolve into peace. For better or worse, you have chosen this path of separate identity, unique being, and the ability to call yourself *I* and have a special name, just for you. Even if others share it, it's still how you identify yourself as unique and separate from others.

> It's a courageous choice to be human, to
> evolve in this manner. At times, the pain of
> separation may be mistaken for the pain of
> living.

Sometimes you don't want to go on living; not necessarily because you are actually contemplating or planning on taking your life, but because there can be a deep weariness to living. There is something inside of you that wants to go, wants to stop the separation; something that you want to rejoin, to become One with. This will only happen when it is meant to happen for each of you. You cannot stop being independent, and you cannot stop being separate simply because you yearn for it. You have made a choice, and the choice to be human must see itself through.

It is a bit like any endeavor you undertake. You may go to a wonderful place for a week, a month, or a year and think you've found paradise. It's so beautiful; you even have thoughts about living there. But after a time, being away, even if where you are is beautiful and wonderful, creates a longing within you to go home, to be in your own space, your own bed, with your own things. It's very much the same. When you choose to embark on a human life, you take a journey. It might *feel* like a long journey, but when you are in Spirit, you'll see it was a quick trip indeed; at some point, you just long to go home.

When the body dies, you rejoin the Soul and the Spirit in harmony. The Soul is the part of the Spirit that always resides within the physical body. When the physical body is done, and the Soul is free to truly be in deeper unity with the Spirit as a whole, it is a marvelous homecoming, a joyous, joyous occasion! There is a larger joining still, where you give up all independence, all experience of being separate and unique; where your consciousness again joins with the One, never again to say *I*, never again to have a name, never again to make individual choices, to exert free will; never again to have personal triumphs or mistakes.

There is something bigger going on in your life. You are called to something greater; not better than, not less than. What I mean by greater, is *expanded*. Your call to awaken is very genuine. It's about knowing yourself, both as the independent Self, and as the One. It's about bridging the gap between the known and the unknown, the seen and the unseen. While, yes, your physical endeavors are important, your *experience* of yourself takes precedence in this life. Your expansion of Self is at the forefront of your being. Your existence, this life of enlightenment, of consciousness, carries with it a responsibility. It is the responsibility to serve. Now, what you serve, and whom you serve, is unique unto you; but know that your ability to awaken has a ripple effect. When you awaken, you help others to awaken as well, so that they—and *you*—are not alone in your awakening.

You are not alone in the process of embracing your life.

There are many misconceptions about the spiritual life—that it is exclusive to only those who have awakened, or that people who are out there doing bad things are not living a spiritual life. This is not true. All who breathe, all who exist, live a spiritual life, because it is all God. Whether one is living deeply in the shadow, or deeply in the light, Spirit is comprised equally of both. There is always a balance, so that you can find your *own* balance between shadow and light, and most profoundly, between human and Spirit and between that which is physical and that which is not. You are emerging as a Divine human capable of extraordinary compassion, extraordinary wisdom, and sometimes, extraordinary pain.

It's normal as a human being, perceiving itself as a separate individual, to want to get what you want, because you are trying to maintain the *I*. You are trying to make sure that you, as the individual, is safe, taken care of, and secure. As adults you are out in the world trying to generate money, create food, clothing, and shelter. Your physical life depends upon these things. It's easy to get caught up in believing that you are separate, that you must create these things for yourself, and that if you don't, no one else will; that if you don't find your soul mate, they'll never come; if you don't start that business, if you don't get that job, if you don't work hard every single day, there will be no food, clothing, shelter; there will be no job, no security, no accolades, no acknowledgment, and no reward.

It's normal to feel this way. You can't help it. You *have* to feel this way. In your perception as a separate being this is absolutely normal, but you are also awake enough to know that there's more, and there's help and support all around you, within you, all the time, helping you see, helping you know, helping you feel, and helping you create. You are already so far on this path of enlightenment, feeling separate, yet connected, feeling singular, yet part of the whole. This already exists within you.

I'm asking you to bring your spiritual path
more to the forefront of your consciousness,

and to focus on it each and every day. I'm
asking you to shift your motivation for
seeking the spiritual path from wanting to
know what it can give you, to wanting to
know what you can discover from it.

This path may not be designed to relieve you from all of your pain. This path may not be designed to bring you exactly what you think you want. What this path is designed to do is to awaken you to yourself. Not to *get*, but to *be*. No matter how hard you try to manipulate the spiritual life, no matter how hard you pray or how much time you spend in meditation, this path may not produce what you want it to produce. What it will bring you is a deeper sense of Self. That's why you stepped onto the path of consciousness. It's why you continue to pursue it, even when you experience pain while on it.

Even though a part of you is very stubborn and continues to ask, *"When is this going to come? When am I going to get this person? When do I get to do this? When is that going to happen?"* Another part of you is just holding your own hand, and whispering, *"Beloved, that's not why we're doing this."* This doesn't necessarily mean that you're here to serve the thousands, either; or write a profound book, be the quintessential healer, or even become a channel. It doesn't mean any of that. But it could. It might.

What comes from focusing on the life force
that is all around you and within you, and
asking, *"How may I serve? How may I
serve?"* When you stop and allow yourself
the profound feeling that moves within
you, of just exactly what it feels like to be

Divine, you find Heaven. It's why you do
anything. It's why you do *all* of it. Not to
get, but to *be*. In these moments, you
experience the profoundness of Self as God.

Yes, you have this extraordinary opportunity to be separate, to call yourself *I*, to make your own decisions. This is but a small facet of the totality of what exists within you and around you. It's not unimportant, but for those of you on this path, it's only a part of what is important. You get to experience such an extraordinarily profound life of connection, which the majority of people do not, simply because it's not yet their time to do so.

You are given a glimpse into a world that people feel may exist only in fairy stories, only in the imagination, and yet—you *feel* it. Yes, you've questioned, and want to know if it's real, if you are making it up. After a while, the answer becomes that it just doesn't matter. You feel it. You feel something extraordinary moving in your life. You feel a current of energy that flows within you and all around you, and gives you an insight and a depth, that if you let it, can be enough. Whatever else happens in your life—positive, wonderful, negative, wonderful—you will take it as it comes; you will feel it as it comes. You are here for more. Never lose sight of that. Never mistake it.

Don't use your chosen path to *get*. Use it to
be.

If you get what you want, wonderful. If you don't, let that be okay too. There is so much within Spirit, that if you don't get what you want in one aspect of your life, you will get it in another. When you remember to expand your mind, your heart, and your feelings, you will remember why you are here and what it is you truly seek in this life. You will be reminded of what deeply matters to you. When the rest is not quite so life or death, you can let go of your worries, and the stress and anxiety that comes from those worries.

You can be easier on yourself and others, and less impatient for things to happen in your time.

Remember that you have come to this life
to discover what it is to *be*; this is what
truly makes you happy, and what will
truly give you peace.

You'll remind yourself of this through your thoughts, your meditations, your prayers, but most importantly, in how you perceive your life.

When you are feeling what you don't have, when you're focused on what you don't have, then you are focused on *getting*. There is nothing wrong with getting, but chances are extremely good that you will never be completely fulfilled with getting. Some things will bring happiness to your life, of course; a sense of achievement, a sense of fulfillment on many levels, absolutely; but to feel the deeper sense of fulfillment that can only be found in the Divine, you must look within yourself.

Your willingness to be, in one sense, will bring you all that you desire, and you will find this within the quiet of yourself. Use all the different tools you've gathered over the years to do whatever it takes to quiet your mind. Don't give up. Don't give up on your being. It can be frustrating to try and move past the chatter, the motivations for getting, for achieving, for feeling important, or gaining something. Why do anything if you can't gain something? This is a very human question. Often, the feeling of being can be elusive, intangible; maybe not quite enough for you to feel you've really gained anything. But look back on your life; you can only tell how far you've come on this journey by looking back.

Looking at how far your life has come will help you understand how much you've truly achieved; regardless of how much money is in the bank, regardless of what you do for work, regardless of who you are with, or not with, in your relationships. Your progress lies in your ability, your willingness to accept that you have chosen a life of enlightenment, to awaken more and more each day, to be conscious of all that you are—laughter, tears, pain.

What frustrates you all, and gets you caught up in *more* pain, is that you are often pursuing a path of enlightenment, spirituality, God, Divine, and *waiting* for the pain to be over. You keep waiting to be completely cured of whatever ails you, and yet it doesn't come. You get focused on why it isn't happening, why you're not having blissful fun, why you still have pain. You then become more focused, and more focused, and more focused, until you forget what *is* happy in your life, what *is* joyful, all the little pleasures in your life. You forget how to have fun.

Sometimes you go days without laughing so become more embroiled in the waiting, working harder, much harder, to try and end all the pain. If you're just a *little* more spiritual, if you meditate just a *few* minutes more, you'll finally get what you want, and be happy every day, all day, for the rest of your life.

No. Pull back. Pull back from your life, your pain, and take a very, very long look at who you are now. Take a look at your extraordinary ability to feel, to open to God, to Spirit, to all the experiences that

you cannot explain, and yet, you've had
them. Acknowledge your courage for
continuing down this path of self-
discovery, that for you defines a spiritual
life.

You keep studying. You keep getting closer and closer to what it is that you want—a feeling of being, of connection, of communion. This is what you need. If you stay focused on that, you will serve God in a capacity that is just right for you. You will have all that you need in this life, and you will know how to make the choices that are before you—small, big, easy, hard—you will know how to make them. Not to get, but to be.

MEDITATION:

Sit quietly and close your eyes.

Take several deep breaths as you move deep into the center of your being.

Let go of the focus on your thoughts. Focus instead on the center of your being.

Call forth from deep within yourself the truth of what I've spoken—not in words, but in feeling. Feel your life as a calling to the greater being. Discover a balance between human and Divine to become divinely human. Feel the call within you.

Feel the very nature and depth of that call. Feel that it comes not from a place of getting, but of being.

Don't think about it—feel it.

Let the calling fill you. Let the clarity of that call leave no room for doubt within you about why you are here, in this life, in this time, doing exactly what you're doing, just now.

Feel the rightness and the peace within that calling.

Feel how deeply your chosen path has brought you what you wanted and needed. What you needed beyond your human life, and within your human life.

Wonderful. Take 3 deep breaths, and with each exhalation, let go of the meditation.

Don't forget to take a birds-eye view of the bigger picture, a more all-encompassing understanding of your life and the choices you've made, and why you've made them. Celebrate your choice, beloved. It is a profound one. Deeply, eternally. I thank you for allowing me to serve you. Be kind to yourselves and each other and know that I love you.

Namaste ~

CHAPTER 14
On my knees

On some level, I recognize that I had a choice to embrace spirituality or reject it, but that is more a thought than a true belief. For me, a spiritual life was a necessity. My addiction was killing me. The disembodied male voice that told me to work on a spiritual program or die was my first tip that I was on the limited choice plan.

Having fewer choices fits my personality. When I go to a restaurant that hands me a menu that's a novel length book, I want to leave. When I'm in a department store, I rarely buy anything. I like boutique living. Having a small number of choices helps me feel less overwhelmed and anxious. So when I was given only two choices—live a spiritual life, or die a desperate, broken person—I was grateful for the simplicity.

For me, a spiritual life doesn't necessarily look a certain way, but it does have a distinct feeling. Plato famously said that the unexamined life was not worth living. The feeling of that statement permeates the whole of my being. It resonates with a vibration that shakes my soul. I can't imagine living any other way.

Yet, on the outside, it may not look to be the case when you compare me to others. I still have all the issues I started out with, but many of them have ceased being issues, and have now become friends. They don't plague me the way they used to.

Yet for all the peace that dwells within me now, putting this book out in the world stirs up all my insecurities and leaves me a shivering mess, cowering in the corner. My shadow tells me in blunt terms that I don't look spiritual enough. I don't sparkle with confidence and a "gosh darn it, I can do it!" attitude. I should look like a yoga goddess with a smoking hot body, a winning smile, eat only pure foods, and live in a state of perpetual serenity so that I become a font of holy wisdom, and sell millions of copies of this book.

Thinking like this doesn't end up working out so well for me. I get royally pissed at myself for rejecting my slightly overweight, potty-mouth, non-yoga doing, crazy, wonderful Self! So I pull a big "F&#* you!" and try to dive head first back into food, or shopping, or fixing my son (or anyone else who might be wandering by).

Before I go too far off the edge, Mother's grace flows through me and I know it's all right to feel exactly the way I'm feeling. She reminds me to hold space for the miracle this thrashing about is creating. If I pick up the food, I'll miss the miracle.

If I write this book with the intention of helping people, it will become a burden; one that I will convince myself I must bear on my own. That belief leads directly to sabotage. I can only answer the call that swirls around inside, seeking an outlet. When I honor and show up for what is being asked of me, I find myself. I can give freely, because I'm full. That's when I get excited about what I'm doing. I feel as though I'm ten years old again and it's the last day of school before summer. The bell rings, and I'm catapulted out of my desk and into joy.

I'm about to make a radical statement—*I don't want to be happy all the time.*

I thought that's what I wanted; what *everyone* wanted. Then I realized, although I love the taste of dark red, ripe cherries, that doesn't mean I want to eat nothing else for the rest of my days! Variety of feeling brings me depth and insight into my existence. I've tried over the years to stay small and invisible because I thought that would keep me safe, and I equate happiness with safety. There is a revolution going on inside of me, and many others I encounter, and I believe Mother Mary is leading the charge. It's about creating a new definition of what being safe means. My *new* safe is knowing that I don't need fixing. *There is nothing wrong with me.* If I want to change something, it's not because I'm *broken*, but because I'm *evolving*.

The last twenty-two years on this spiritual path have not been paved with unicorns and rainbows. Just after Mother came to me and we began our journey together, I relapsed back into the black hole of my food addiction. I spent the better part of a year trying to crawl back out of that hole. There is nothing worse than having gotten out from under a demoralizing obsession, only to be thrown back in. Before recovering from my eating disorder, I didn't know any other existence; but to have experienced relief and found life again, only to lose it, was devastating. My relapse was momentous. I learned humility. I needed to experience life on my knees in order to accept my union with Divine Mother.

Through Mother Mary's grace, I didn't give up on my connection with Her. I was able to sit with Her every morning and weep, wail, complain, wade through my self-pity, and arrive at a place inside that allowed me to do the exercises She asked me to do. Mother called this our transcendence work. It brought us closer and provided the space for me to run away and return, as often as I needed to. Like a stray cat, I let Her care for me until it finally felt safe to stay.

My food hell brought me to my knees in daily surrender. It was here my humility was born. It became the key ingredient in my spiritual life. I soaked in the knowing that when left to my own devices I'm a wrecking ball—tearing things down faster than I can build them. When I try to do anything in isolation, clinging to the belief that I know what's best, I'm miserable. With Mother's constant presence, the window to freedom from my obsession with food finally opened again, and I dove through it like a cheerleader at the Super Bowl.

That year stripped me bare. The battle that raged between my eating disorder and my desire to get out from under the obsession left my castle walls in ruins. The childish belief that I could cure my addiction just by wishing it so had to be smashed. I wanted to be the one to fix me; I wanted to be the answer; not God or anyone else. That way I could appear superior, strong, and together. That's the stuff my walls were made of. At the time, these were my defenses. If I looked like I was doing well, then I was. I was convinced that being Mother's channel offered me immunity to all addiction and suffering. My relapse had me facing my constant need to have things my way. When I asked Her why She wouldn't cure me, She answered, *"Why would I take from you the one thing that will ensure you always return to me?"* Fair enough. I knew I couldn't recover without Her. That made me willing to let go, and not rebuild what I had managed to break free from.

There were enough of my walls left standing that I could hide behind them if I needed to, yet now there were windows that opened to the light of Spirit as well. I feel alive when I follow Her loving guidance, even if it leads me to pain. She taught me that my addiction was an inner barometer. When I denied my problems and hid from people, I wanted to overeat. When I stayed close to Her and took positive action, I didn't. The accuracy of my barometer is one hundred percent. If She had taken that from me through no effort of my own, I would have missed lifetimes worth of experience. The experience of living an examined life is filled with variety. That means pain along with joy, and everything in between. I thought I wanted a life free of pain, but I discovered that to be a sterile life, devoid of depth and intimacy.

I live my spiritual life for myself. I'm not a Sherpa burdened with guilt, trying to make it up the cultural mountain of maintaining a spiritual image. I have been relieved of the timeline to achieve. I awaken in small increments that are like aftershocks, rippling out from the original earthquake that had brought me to consciousness. My humility shows me that is enough; and when I bask in Mother's grace, I feel that I'm enough.

This book is my love letter to Mother. While it's primarily written in Her words, they came through me. A master of the unseen recently reminded me that no matter what, I have shown up for what has been asked of me. While that may not sound like much of a compliment, to me it was monumental. I need my spiritual life. I can't live without it. Left alone, I don't want to show up for anything or anyone; least of all myself. This writing process has stirred my pot. I'm currently cultivating a friendship with the part of me that wants to hit delete and run. What is before me, is not so much to write this book, but to love all of me that's writing it.

Mother is my Master. I am Her Beloved. This is my joy. Humility and acceptance are my new safety. What comes will come. Who I am within what comes to me, decides my experience. I choose to follow, because it is my privilege to do so.

CHAPTER 15
The shadow within

We looked briefly at your shadow in previous chapters, but now I wish to focus on and explore your shadow in more depth. It's not only your own shadow that lives within, but the collective shadow. This affects you from the outside, where mankind's shadows come together to create the collective shadow, which you're a part of and must face. I hope I can bring you some different thoughts and possibilities, as well as a broadening and deepening perspective in regards to your own and the collective's shadow.

What is most important to understand right away is that the shadow exists within as an extension of the light. They are not opposites, as much as different sides of the same coin, so to speak. In this reality, in your awakened existence, dark and light coexist in a way that is inseparable. They are designed to work together to help you create an experiential awareness of creation.

> The shadow adds depth and dimension to light. It creates a desire to journey, to know, understand, and experience revelation.

If your physical life were all light, as your existence was before you chose to embark on this extraordinary human journey, light would be all that you knew. As such, it's impossible to create *or* discover the desire to explore that experience. When you are fully in the light, there's no need to discover. There's a feeling of contentment and complacency; not that this is harmful, but it can become stagnant. And creation is never stagnant.

If you're an artist and you draw or paint, you recognize that it's the shading, or the shadowing, that brings forward the image. Without shading, you wouldn't have the perspective of depth when you looked at a drawing or painting. So, too, shadowing does with life. Without the shadow, you're not able to create depth. You're not able to bring the imagery of your life forward. It's through your eyes that your brain perceives images, using both the light and the shadow. It's how you perceive life. You can never separate the two. It's not so much that their interconnectedness creates different shades of grey, as it is that their interconnectedness creates color and an abundance of depth, which is achieved through discovery and the desire to look beyond and go deeper.

It usually starts out with two elements. One, a very heavy dose of curiosity; you can't really embark on a spiritual path if you're not curious. You may not be curious about everything in life, but for whatever reason, you're curious about human beings, and why things and people are the way they are, why they feel the way they feel, and why things happened the way they did in order for you to have the life that you have.

The second element that drives your sense of discovery is pain. Pain is a deep motivator. The desire to relieve one's self of pain is one of the greatest, if not *the* greatest, motivating factor in humans. This has allowed you the ability to stretch beyond what is in your immediate life, and delve into the deeper parts of your unknown Self. This is how creation takes place.

There's a lot of creating that can sometimes feel as though it's happening by habit. Things keep happening in the way that they've always happened. But then there are other aspects to creating that come when people are deeply curious and deeply driven to find relief from pain. It can drive people in science, technology, business, and interpersonal relationships deeply into spirituality. That's not to say that everyone who is creative and curious is in pain, but the vast majority are.

You create a life for yourself, but at the start of your journey it may feel like others created it, as if the will of others was imposed upon you. Yes, you were influenced by both the collective light and shadow of others, but you came individually with your own personality, the part of you that is intrinsically *you*, and cannot be swayed by external manipulations, education, or outside forces. It's the part that you came with, will die with, and will live with every moment in-between. This is the part of you that chooses how you perceive all the influences in your life, and ultimately creates your perspective.

While your shadow is responsible for much of your pain, in truth, it's one of your greatest assets in this life. It's that which highlights light to such a degree that you can recognize it. There's an intuitive Self that knows right from wrong and can recognize good from bad, but it's really your shadow that shades the light in such a way that it stands out. It becomes two and three dimensional, making it easier for you to recognize and know inside your being, that yes, this is the right way to go.

In the beginning it may seem as though it's the light that alone illuminates the path, but without the shadow around the light, you couldn't *see* the path. If there was no shade, you would be *blinded* by light! You wouldn't see *anything*. They work together to allow you to explore and move ever closer to your Spirit and mind, your comfort, and your willingness to surrender old understandings of security, but at a pace that is set by you.

Without shadow, there would be no understanding of light. As a Soul, shadow helps you to experience light in a precious way, so it doesn't become just an everyday thing. Because it may not be the thing you are saturated in every moment of every day, it becomes precious and something that you never take for granted any more. It becomes so important that you focus more and more of your energies on it. You want to receive it and give it to others so that they too may share in the light, and may have both light and shadow illuminating their path. Someday your Soul will desire complete Oneness again—only then will there be only light.

> *Your entire journey brings understanding*
> *of how precious your light existence truly*
> *is.*

There is a saying in your culture that you don't really appreciate something until it's gone, and if only you were so lucky to have it come back to you, you'd never take it for granted again. This is how newness is always brought into creation—new perspectives, new gratitude, a new way of experiencing light—things that before you began this particular journey in human form were assumed.

Your shadow is a friend to you on your journey, because if offers you shelter, in a way. Imagine that it's a very hot, sunny day, you're sweating, and your skin begins to feel as though it's burning. You move into the shade— Ahh... instant relief. It's a place to rest; a familiar place that has been with you a long time. The intensity of the light can be overwhelming, and is why you don't discover Spirit, and then run headlong into it to be completely and utterly consumed by it. You step into the light but can only take so much, so you step back into the cool shade. Then you move out into the light again. It's not exactly black and white because when you're in the shade, there is still much light; you're not in the deepest, blackest darkness, just simply in the shade.

There are Souls in your world who are new to the human evolutionary process. These are the ones who are very deep into the blackness, and are just leaving the light to embrace the shadow, beginning the very long journey back from darkness to shadow, then into the shade, and eventually fully into the light again. As you discover the nuances, the facets, of your shadow and light, and how they are sometimes so similar in feeling (barely a breath separates them), you begin to understand the stronger aspects of your shadow, the parts of yourself that keep you separate from the light, and exactly what the shadow is.

The shadow is that which gives you the experience of feeling separate from God, separate from light, separate from the eternal bliss of Oneness. Ultimately, from an energetic or spiritual standpoint, you are never separate, but the feeling is very real. So I can't say to you that the separation *isn't* real, because it *feels* real. You must recognize that there are things that you are feeling in this life that are very real to you, but may not be facts of a universal nature.

The shadow allows you the ability, the desire, the desperate need, and the curiosity to dive into life, creation, and spirituality.

Living can be very messy, stop and start, one step forward and five steps back—but sometimes, ten steps forward and only one step back. There's a flow that comes, a rhythm that is yours and yours alone. It will never fully look or feel like anyone else's.

This flow, this rhythm, is the dance of dark and light. There is no hard separation, even from those who are new and are deep into the darkest part of shadow. They can be surrounded by light as an extraordinary reminder, and within themselves they will still experience the joy and rapture of living, even if that joy and rapture comes through and is created by darkness.

One of the greatest challenges to a spiritual seeker is to free the mind from a black and white viewpoint; good and bad, this and that, them and us. It's hard to blur the edges, it's hard to conceptualize that everything that's going on is of God. And while this life is extremely important—this world, this *planet* is extremely important—you must discover what is important to *you*. Meaning, it's not so much what happens in your life or world, but quite literally, how you make the journey, from start to finish.

At this point, when you're in the shadow, in the shade resting, you are being asked to find respect for your shadow and to honor it. It's something that will always be with you as a human being. Even those who are quite illuminated and at the end of their human evolution, and who are ready not to come back as humans anymore, will still have a shadow until the very end of their human existence. It's part of being human.

It is the shadow that gives you compassion.
Everyone thinks that compassion, one of
the greatest forms of love, comes from light,
but it is not so. Compassion is born chiefly
from your shadow. (Of course, if we go back
to the original premise that it's all light,
then yes, compassion also comes from light,
but here I am speaking of your human

existence.) Compassion comes from
experience. Your ability to see someone
else's shadow, to recognize their suffering,
and regardless of what you personally
think about them, feel kindness,
understanding, and love for what they are
going through.

Why does the shadow build compassion? Because once you have experienced something deeply painful yourself, you can relate to other's pain, so you feel loving compassion towards them. If not for your shadow, for your experiences of pain and suffering, you would never be able to extend compassion to another human being. It simply would not be possible.

Look at the story of the man from your history who was known as my son—Christ, Yeshua, Yahweh, the Beloved One—in terms of myth or cultural teachings. If you look at his life in terms of compassion, then God sent his son, his energy, his Spirit, to take on human form. Now, this individual had never been human before. This individual was first and last in that life, and only in that life. According to the popular teaching, he came to live, teach, and spread a message; and in his death, to relieve humanity of the burden of sin, or what I call your shadow.

What was the point of Jesus becoming a
human being? By becoming human, it was
easier to learn compassion than any other
way. To come and experience being human,
even for just a short time, gave him a
shadow—a shadow that gave him depth,
perspective, compassion, and empathy. So

now, his Spirit, his Christ energy, is able to
serve humanity deeply, because this energy
now understands conflict, doubt, fear,
judgment, pain, and betrayal—all the
things that you suffer and struggle with.
How can we serve you, truly and deeply
serve you, if we have not been one of you?

There are energies that serve humanity, but have not
taken human form; they perform a different service; still
necessary, but not as based in compassion. Compassion is a
deeply human, very particular aspect of love. Energies such
as Yeshua and me, can serve with unconditional
compassion because we are no longer human, nor are we
tied deeply to the shadow of being human. But we
understand absolutely and completely what it is to have a
shadow—not only how difficult it feels, but how its purpose
is to move us to enlightenment. Without shadow, you could
not become enlightened.

What I'm trying to convey to you, my
beloved ones, is that you must work *with*
your shadow, not against it. Do not reject
your shadow. Do not wish to separate from
your shadow. Do not wish to get rid of your
shadow—because you cannot. Your
evolution is an absolute transformation of
the shadow into bright light. There will be
less and less shade—but as there is less
shade, you will become more and more
comfortable in the intense white light,
which strips away everything you are and

leaves you utterly exposed. Yes, it's glorious
in one sense, but it's also deeply frightening
in another. You will still need shade. If you
learn to have compassion for your Self by
getting to know your shadow, you will
have a deeper understanding of why it
exists in the first place.

I am giving you words. I am offering you a new perspective; or for some of you, just a slightly deeper perspective. You must face, explore, understand, and feel your own shadow. It's not going to be the same as anyone else's, just as your light will always be unique as well. How the shadow and light play together, is the shading in your life that brings forth the image that is *you*. This *you* must explore. If you are fighting your shadow, you internally desire rejection.

Self-loathing is a rejection of your shadow. You fight your shadow when you think that some part of you is broken, or unworthy of existing. This is when you actually give in to your shadow to such a degree that you allow it to overwhelm the light. Be careful of this, because if you allow the shadow to overwhelm the light too much and too often, you will begin to resent the light, the shadow, and everything and everyone. You will begin to blame parts of your life that are not actually responsible for your experience.

Yes, your shadow helps you set the pace of your enlightenment, of the transition from shadow to light, but your shadow is not the sole and exclusive consciousness that is alive within you.

When you abdicate your responsibility to
consciousness for your shadow because you

are too frightened, don't want to deal, feel
too tired, or too this or too that, then you
must recognize that this is *your* choice, and
the shadow will take over because you
asked it to.

When you give over your choices to your shadow, then your shadow provides for you. It provides depression, fear, and feelings of inadequacy, and tells you you'll never have enough, rather than focusing on what you *do* have. All of these things are a part of the depth, of what gives texture and beauty to your life, and lets you understand compassion deeply, so that you can feel love, love, love, love.

If you are not awake, and if you are not
participating in your own life, then you are
abdicating to your shadow. That's all right,
but you must be aware of this, and you
must take personal responsibility. This is
very important.

When you are on the spiritual path, awakening yourself to light, shadow, and the consciousness that's going on all around and within you, then you accept a responsibility to gain your sight, so to speak. You become able to see beyond and feel more deeply, see more deeply, and to comprehend a greater depth. This is a gift, a very extraordinary gift, and with it comes responsibility.

As a result, sensitivities that you may have had your whole life, finally feel as though they've found an outlet, and you begin to understand that this is *why* you are so very sensitive—because you are awakening to yourself. Without sensitivity, you could not awaken. But when you accept the gift of awakening, know that it comes with responsibility.

When you do not take responsibility for yourself, you create problems for yourself.

Now here is an interesting thought—so many of you, when thinking of taking responsibility for yourself, think in terms of all the bad things that have happened, and believe that you've caused all of your pain and misery. It's hard for you to take responsibly for the great things in your life, though. Not that you are creating any of it alone in a vacuum, of course; you are co-creating it with all that is around you, including other people, all of which comes together as one life.

You've been given something precious, a window into your own life, your own being, and through that window you can see much farther into the lives of others, and into life itself; into the heart of God. Cherish that gift, and know that as a sensitive individual you will be asked to go to extraordinary lengths, where others may not be, in order to safeguard your sensitivity, your ability to know.

Your shadow does not fight you, but it will always move into a default pattern if you don't reset your settings. If the shadow has been put in charge of certain things all your life, and you don't make considerable effort to change and shift, you will inevitably go back to default. Again, this is perfectly normal and absolutely fine, but recognize that it's something that you are doing, and have compassion for yourself as you're doing it. Sometimes when you do things that cause you pain again and again, it's a signal that you're not yet ready to move beyond.

> Blaming others, and especially blaming
> yourself, is the one default that you have
> relied upon in your shadow, and I
> encourage you to heal this. Take the time to
> write about and explore how you blame

*yourself. Self-forgiveness on a continual
basis is founded on compassion. A deep
understanding of why you do the things
you do may not change things, but it will
help you with compassion and empathy for
yourself and others.*

Your shadow is never going to take over unless you allow it, unless you need it to, unless you ask it to, or unless you abdicate responsibility and stay in default mode. Recognize that the shadow and light, both outside of you and inside of you, are working together to show you the world you live in and who you really are; not so you can judge it, blame it, or run away from it, but so you can be alive within it—not just existing, not just drifting through your days—but gloriously alive.

*To feel deeply alive is to be awake.
Your passions, desires, dreams, and
creativity are all about being alive. It's
your willingness to accept your shadow, to
honor your shadow, and to work with your
shadow in order to understand yourself
better, that will make the greatest
difference in your life, and in your
enlightenment.*

When I say *work with your shadow*, I don't necessarily mean to feed your depression or self-loathing. *No.* To work with your shadow is to feel these things, to know that for now they have a place in your life, but to feel the light there just as strongly. Discover the shadow and light working together as one, unified within you, so that you might understand yourself more deeply—not to judge, not to blame, not to reject—but to feel, to experience.

When you allow the dark and light to work together, they paint images for you that stand out and bring you an experiential understanding of Self. It's not just about knowledge, but experience as well, because through experience comes wisdom. It is wisdom that brings about compassion. It is wisdom that awakens you to life.

If you're not feeling so very alive, if you're feeling as though you are drifting, that you've lost your passion, or maybe that you never had it, then it's time for you to commune with your shadow.

> *Discover an ally where you once thought*
> *there was only an enemy that must be*
> *defeated at all costs, but who is in fact the*
> *author of most, if not all, of the*
> *illumination that takes place in your life.*
> *It's the shadow that is at the heart of*
> *revelation for human beings.*

It's normal to fear your shadow. If you come to your shadow filled with light, compassion, understanding, and empathy, with your hands out and open in friendship rather than clenched in combat, you will discover that your perception of Self will shift dramatically.

> *All your default settings will begin to reset*
> *because you understand that where you are*
> *in your life right now, with self-loathing,*
> *depression, blaming, and judgment, does*
> *not represent you as a whole anymore. It*
> *may have at one time, and a part of you*

*may still resonate with that as strongly as
it once did. That's to let you know where
you still need to dive in. That's where you
need to pull the light and shadow into your
whole consciousness. You move deeply into
depression, and what is there for you? You
move deeply into judgment, and what is
there for you? You move deeply into self-
loathing, and what is there for you?*

Energetically, don't always depend on self-exploration
to translate into words feelings such as self-loathing, blame
towards your parents, or judgments about what you think is
wrong with your life. Move beyond the words.

*Your shadow and light truly create your
existence and are the creative forces within
you. Let them show you the things that
bring you pain, fear, or sadness. Let them
give you an experience without words,
because words are only a small part of the
total understanding.*

Until you delve into shadow and understand it, you will
not move it or change it. Through your understanding, you
can take different actions. As you take different actions,
your shadow changes, transforms, and becomes something
else. As you rest in the shade, it becomes a little lighter, and
a little lighter, and a little lighter. As the light grows and
intensifies and the heat is more intense, your body is
perfectly acclimated and feels right and good, so you don't
have to seek the darker parts of the shade anymore.

The shadow within, will always speak to,
and draw to you, the shadow that is around
you. You will find that when you focus on
the shadow that is outside—society, politics,
religion, science, business, and other things
that bring you the most pain, rage, and the
deepest anger—there will be an element to
these things that mimic the shadow within
you that is clamoring for your attention.
The very thing that you've set on default
will keep triggering and triggering and
triggering you, over and over again.

The shadow within will call to the external shadow. What stands out to you in your outward perceptions is that which requires your attention within; that which causes you the most pain in your life. It may not be an exact reflection, but whatever triggers you from the outside, be sure there is a similar aspect of your shadow that is ready to be transformed into light. It's calling for your attention over and over and over again, and trying to bring you those elements of compassion, curiosity, and pain, that you need to explore.

Discover what it is about the things outside of yourself that trigger you. Find that element within your own shadow, then take your light *and* shadow, your strong and beautiful Self, and explore that part of your shadow with its cooperation; for revelation of, and understanding and compassion for, all that you are, and all that you will become.

MEDITATION:

Sit quietly and close your eyes. Take several deep breaths, exhaling fully. Settle deeply into the center of your being, the place of stillness, the place where oneness is known.

Now, using your intention and breath, call to your shadow. You may feel it both inside and outside your body. Your shadow is a part of the whole of your Spirit, which surrounds and infuses your human body. Try not to focus on any one aspect of your shadow. Just call forth its presence.

Let go of what you think you know about your shadow and allow yourself to just feel it in this moment. Even if your past experience is based in the positive, let it go and be with your shadow now. Let it expand in your awareness. Allow yourself to feel its depth, to feel its relationship to light, to feel its relationship to you. Feel the light within your shadow and the shadow within your light. Feel the interconnectedness.

If you are able, find gratitude for your shadow now—just let it be there—for the wonder of all that has been, is now, and will be illuminated and revealed in your life. The deeper you know your shadow, the deeper your compassion will be for yourself and all others that come into your life, whether personally or just through your notice of their deeds in the world. Your shadow to their shadow, as you are but One shadow; your light to their light, as you but are One light; your being to their being, as you are but One being; One in spirit; One in life.

Now slowly, gently, let go of the focus on your shadow. Come back to your breathing. Feel the breath, and only the breath, moving in and out of your body.

This is what it feels like to work with your shadow. You don't necessarily have to direct your shadow. Just be present with it, to feel how extraordinary a role it plays in your life. To accept and to honor it, to let it have your focus from time to time, that is how you honor it. The more you feel this, the easier it will be to go from default to new places within, and to become more comfortable in the light, to acclimate to the light, and to accept and honor that. As you honor your shadow, and that becomes the honoring of your light, you honor yourself. When you honor yourself in all that you are, you find unity, passion, and a deep sense of being alive.

Take three deep breaths, and on the exhalation, let go of the meditation. You may slowly open your eyes.

I thank you for allowing me to serve you. Rejoice in your compassion, as you rejoice in your humanity. Know that I love you deeply.

Namaste ~

CHAPTER 16
Mr. hyde

I love my shadow; sometimes because I have to (like putting up with an annoying sibling), but most of the time because I want to. I also *like* my shadow. That's quite a leap from the intense self-loathing I used to feel. I'm fascinated by the human experience. What motivates us supplies a never-ending source for exploration. My fascination doesn't come from a scientific place, but more a companionable one. In short, I need to know other people's shadows in order to appreciate mine. Here are the things I adore about my own shadow:

1. My sense of humor
2. My depth of compassion
3. My empathy for all life
4. My boundaries
5. My grit
6. Freedom from perfection

I would rather explore myself and others through films like *Fight Club* and *Silver Linings Playbook*, than *The Secret* or *What the Bleep Do We Know!?* Anne Lamott, with her bold honesty and naked sense of humor, is my favorite spiritual author because she's not trying to teach me anything; she's just sharing her life with me. I'm the first to admit that I may have some slight *DON'T TELL ME WHAT TO DO* issues. So for me, a being like Mother is who I need to access my spiritual guidance from.

When it comes to other humans, learning from their

experience, especially when it's offered with humor, reaches through my fog of denial like nothing else. Accepting my shadow, allows me to know the things I once perceived as wrong or bad are so much richer in content than I am able to perceive. Knowing that gives me permission to engage with things that will touch my truth center, light up my epiphanies, and trigger my sense of awe. My shadow has released me from the burden of needing to be right. If Mother's teachings weren't practical, logical, and infused with love and grace the way they are, I wouldn't be interested. She loves all of me as a whole being. Her unconditional love has made it possible for me to embrace my shadow and shrink the gap between my good girl and my bad girl.

Acceptance of all of me is critical to my salvation. If I have it, I embrace it. I love my ego. How? Because Mother loved it first. She is one of the few teachers out in the world who praises the ego and brings me the knowing that I am not a mistake. I have no problems. I have no issues. My perception is that I *do* have problems and issues; and the reactions that stem from my perceptions are the source of my pain. How is it possible to love myself while rejecting my ego, the very thing that allows me to individuate as a human being?

My friendship with my shadow began with my channeling of Mother Mary. She told me when we first began that She wouldn't ask anything of me that She wouldn't ask of others. I was relieved to know that the bar would be set equally, because I had so little faith in my own ability to show up. I looked for any excuse the first few years not to channel. I was tired, my stomach hurt, not enough people were coming, anything to talk myself out of showing up. I had to claim my channeling for myself before a shift in my perception could take place. That day came by digging deep and finding a sliver of willingness to do one more channeling, and then one more, until I became comfortable in my own skin, now that I was sharing it with Mother.

I felt like Sisyphus with that damn boulder. Mine was made out of fear; unbreakable and as heavy as a '59 Buick. When it stopped being solely about how many were coming or not coming to a channeling, how successful I would be or how badly I would fail, it became an exercise in showing up for myself. Like a loyal hound awaiting its master with a doggy dance and a slobbery kiss, my shadow was waiting for me. I was expecting Mr. Hyde, with evil intent and cruel words. It turns out that my shadow just craved my attention, with a desperation born of constant rejection and neglect.

I didn't even know I had a shadow until my awakening to consciousness. I believed everyone and everything else was responsible of robbing me of a good life. Once I came face to face with it, I couldn't run away fast enough. Its enthusiasm for me was unnerving. My shadow felt like broken glass in my stomach, because at first I didn't know what to do with it. Then Mother gently said, *"Just be with her, beloved."*

Nope, that was too simple. I still needed something to blame. I fashioned it into Mr. Hyde, evil intent and all. I chose to perceive my shadow a malevolent force within me, constantly setting me up for failure and humiliation. It worked beautifully as my new target for blame.

Imagine my horror when Mother told me in Her most patient, loving voice that my shadow and I were to become the best of friends. *"NO!"* was my first, second, and third response. Why couldn't I channel a normal entity that taught that the ego was the enemy, and that our shadow had to be destroyed by our light? What happened to the good old

American way of kicking ass and taking no prisoners? I wanted to blow some stuff up and live happily ever after. *"No, Beloved,"* was always Her response. *"There is another way."* Chest heaving in resignation, I would respond, *"Fine. What do I do?"*

Those moments were pure grace. It wasn't long before I caught fleeting glimpses of my shadow being loved by Her as much as my light. Sure, I would rationalize, She *has* to love all of me; She's the *Mother*. But that's not what I was feeling. There wasn't even a hint that She was only tolerating my shadow. True love was present. It wasn't the kind of pity-love you bestow on someone you don't really like and know isn't long for this world. It was a permanent, abiding kind of love.

How can that be? I clung to that question like an ill-tempered dog with a bone it refuses to let go of, even when something tastier is presented. *"Let's not leave any part of you behind, alright, Beloved one?"* When Her voice washed through me with those words, I was willing to try.

Mother taught me to look upon my shadow as a parent would look upon a child. With that one suggestion, I was able to see my shadow's reactions, actions, and feelings in a new light. It became easy to see that I had some serious arrested development. My shadow seemed to be stuck at around six or seven years old. It wanted everything done for it, with no expenditure of effort on its part, while doing everything its own way in its own time, with no room for helpful suggestions from another source. It felt exhausting, like arguing with a toddler.

Like a shadow on the wall, Mr. Hyde was only a *projection* of evil. It was my rejection of Self that was really hurting me. I came to the understanding that I could have all my feelings and perceptions no matter what, but what I did with them was what determined the quality of my life. I used to tell my son that he could get mad, but he couldn't bash his friends over the head with his toys. Now, I also don't bash people over the head with my blame as often as I used to. Not only did it hurt them, but their hurt brought pain to my heart; my shadow didn't like that feeling, so we decided to do it Mother's way.

I am my shadow. I don't feel it as a separate being or energy so much anymore. Allowing this shift in perspective has had the most profound effect on my Self-love. When I'm not practicing the illusion of separation, I can better discern my needs. In unity, I feel better able to support myself no matter what I'm experiencing.

It was my humor that gave me the greatest insight into my shadow. Sharing with others the absurdity of rushing at midnight into Ralph's grocery store in Hollywood (affectionately called Rock and Roll Ralph's by the late night zombies that shopped there), desperate to find the exact right cookies that would complete me as a person, taught me not to take myself so seriously. My shadow could find humor in just about any situation, no matter how dark. Having gallows humor saved my life. The intuitive revelation that it stemmed equally from my shadow and light, helped me to see that some of my other favorite qualities had come from my shadow. Like all things, and everyone, I am a mixture of the elements that formed in such a way as to be me; one of many, yet still unique.

CHAPTER 17
Miracles

Miracles are that which is unexpected in one's life, and yet somehow expected, known, looked for, or hoped for. When they come, there's a sense of connection to something far greater than you. They help you remember who you really are. Miracles allow you the freedom to go beyond what holds you in bondage.

Miracles are the everyday experiences that show you beyond a doubt that you have purpose in this life.

Some miracles have a synchronicity that is unmistakable. Those are the most obvious ones. They're the ones you pay the closest attention to and remember. They're the ones that grab your attention even when you're looking the other way. But now, I want to focus on the subtle miracles; those things that occur in life that you're not used to acknowledging as miracles; the things you take for granted.

I have spoken often of gratitude, the importance of focusing on it, and how gratitude can dramatically change your reality. Particularly, if for whatever reason you're focused on what is *not* happening in your life, or what is negative and problematic, gratitude can shift the focus onto what you *do* have, and ultimately, how abundant your life will be no matter what is occurring.

Miracles go even farther than that. The energy of miracles has an enthusiasm for life that gratitude can kick start. The miracle creates a sense of excitement and adventure, the sense that anything could be waiting for you a minute from now, an hour from now, or a day from now. If you pay attention, they'll come. They're going to come anyway, but if you're not paying attention, you'll miss so many! How many of you have looked back on your past, not with regret, but with a sense of awe at how many wonderful things had happened. However, when you were there, it didn't necessarily feel that way.

Miracles, if you allow them to, can keep your attention. They can keep you focused on and in a state of awe. Life is so much more than just a sense of good or bad, right or wrong, dark or light. If you think about the words that you commonly use to describe your life, they are often a little dry or clinical.

> I would like you to introduce a little more
> verve into your vocabulary when talking
> about your day, your experiences, and your
> life. What is your life, if not a constant
> series of miracles? Is it not a miracle that
> you breathe in and out?

As you grow in your awareness, and as it deepens, you'll get a sense that you are seeing God more and more; not only in the people around you, but in your environment and the events that transpire within your environment. You will begin to see God, even in people and situations that you may not agree with or relate to. For each of you this will be a little different. You may begin to feel a strong energy that flows through everything.

For many of you, not seeing this, not paying attention, is becoming harder and harder to do. You're working harder and harder, and longer and longer, to maintain density and denial. One of my favorite human behaviors is how you explain miracles away, and that after all these years there's a part of you that still believes in coincidences. It's becoming more of a struggle to maintain your doubt, to maintain your distance, and to maintain your lack of enthusiasm. It's harder to be cool. It's harder to be cynical. It's harder to be sarcastic. It's harder to maintain the distance that you think makes you look very put together and intellectual, because every day these miracles are drawing you in, and every day you feel more of the energy of excitement within them. I would love to see you allow yourself to experience the excitement.

When was the last time you got jump-on-the-bed excited? Shouting out loud, laughing, excited about something or someone new? I'm not talking about unobtainable recognition. I see that you feel you have too much stress and too many problems, difficulties, heartaches, and confusion, but at this point if I were you, I would challenge that belief down to its very core. I'd like for you to start thinking about how much time and energy you spend trying to maintain a lack of excitement about your life. The way that you do this is by creating or focusing on the endeavors you choose to struggle in. This is when change can occur; when you realize how much time and energy is spent on thinking that something isn't going to happen, rather than that it is.

The miracle is that it's happening all around you, all the time. All that you actually need, it turns out, is to be what you really want to be. It's all here for you.

Where do you place your focus? Do you focus on the belief that you're the one shutting miracles out, or that you're the one that can let them in? This will be the

difference between having an abundance of
miracles in your life, or just the occasional
miracle in your life.

I'm putting this in very simple terms. A part of you knows how complex your beliefs and problems are. I've said it for many years, in many different ways, but a part of you still won't believe me when I tell you how simple things are. You have spent enough time digging into the past, and you're very aware of your issues, problems, and difficulties. As a matter of fact, most of you can recite them quite easily when asked.

Now is the time in your life to stay focused on allowing. You've had so many miracles in your life thus far that you can feel when you're allowing yourself to receive them. You know what's coming is for the very best. When the belief rises within you that says, wait, it's too much, you can't allow it, and have to put the brakes on, please ask yourself what you're trying so hard to control. Your life is happening all around you all the time. You don't have to put the brakes on. There's no such thing. Brakes are an illusion. You will always go at the pace you need to go. It's never gone any other way. Regardless of how strongly you feel you must try to control what's coming to you, you cannot.

You can't control what you receive; only
what you perceive.

When you allow miracles, you'll know each day that your life *is* the miracle, so that no matter what happens in your day, you'll be grateful for it. You'll begin to see God more clearly and deeply, and in a way that goes far beyond your finite existence. You'll move into conscious contact with what is all around you, and what is moving through your life and everyone else's.

> I'm asking you to begin treating yourself,
> thinking of yourself, and feeling yourself
> as the miracle. Not just *a* miracle, but *the*
> miracle. Your perception is within you, and
> everything that you perceive comes from
> the inside out. If you are the miracle, then
> everything you perceive is a miracle. Start
> small, with your breath, your heartbeat,
> the blood that flows through your body;
> with your ability to recall a name from
> childhood; your ability to recognize what is
> around you; your ability to say, *I Am*; the
> ability to perceive your own unique
> existence, your sentient thoughts; the
> ability to relate to others in a way that sets
> you apart. This is the miracle of
> communication.

Even if you're just sending a text message, notice how extraordinary it is that you can even participate in something like that. And I don't just mean that you can buy the device, although that's a wonderful thing to be able to do. But the act of communicating itself is a miracle, regardless of how you do it.

Be careful. Your society is becoming even less excited about its own existence. It's easy to become a part of that, to feel bored. On one level, I understand it; and on another, it's astonishing that there can even be boredom, period. It's common in your culture to encourage people not to get too excited, not to be too happy, not to be too sad, either, and not too angry, not too grateful, and certainly not too devotional. Take it all with a grain of salt, or not at all. As usual, I'm asking you to do the opposite, to take a different road. Recognize that the miracle you're a part of is the extraordinary society of individuals you live with on your planet. Know that as an individual, you can choose to play it cool, or you can choose to become excited about your very existence.

> If you look closely enough, you'll find the miracle in the pain and chaos. You'll find the miracles when you walk through the fire. And when you do, the fire will crack you open so you can plant seeds, start something new, and leave something of value to those that come after you.

There will always be the grace of miracles in your life, no matter what you believe, no matter if you look for them or not. They will always be there. Why not see them everywhere, rather than just here and there? Forget about what others think of your excitement. You're growing away from the desire and need for outside approval. You're learning to make your own choices, and to live your own life in the way you feel drawn to live it. Let that show a little more on the outside. Don't keep it so much to yourself.

It's not so much about sharing words of wisdom, as it is sharing the energy of miracles. Let yourself be the miracle. This is all you would ever have to teach to anyone. You would never even have to open your mouth. Everyone would know and feel it. It's already happening inside. Just let it out. Share it. This is too important to keep a secret. There may be a voice inside that says you don't have much to be excited about, that there's not much going on, or that your life is boring and you do pretty much the same thing every day. Acknowledge that voice. Love that voice. Say, *"Thank you for sharing,"* to that voice. But keep looking for the miracles anyway, because you already know they're there.

When you meet others that seem to be genuinely excited about life, do you find that at times they irritate you? No one is going to raise a hand on that one. When you meet people who are doing things that drive you crazy, it's generally because *their* negativity is *your* negativity. What they do bugs you because you do it too. What you also may not recognize, is that when you meet people who have what you want and are joyous, it will bother you. You will convince yourself that they're phony, that no one could be that excited or upbeat or happy about life, and that they're obviously in denial. I'd like for you to sit yourself down and have a nice little talk with yourself about that. *"Hmm, what do they have that I need for myself? Is it envy that's speaking?"*

Mark my words, there's an enthusiasm that you're going to have a harder and harder time squelching and keeping quiet. The more you discover about what's inside, the more you're going to realize that it may not even be a passion for a specific thing, like a new career or hobby. Yes, it can be all of that, but it's much, much more—it's an enthusiasm for your life, for yourself. You don't have to have a big life change to feel it.

It's the kind of thing that's dependent on nothing but you being; not *doing*, just *being*. This is the great miracle that I've come to tell you about; that *you* are the miracle just as you are. Don't wait for a *doing* miracle. You will always *do* things. But to walk out into the world *as* the miracle, *being* the miracle, now that's where you're going! That's the dharma for all of you, individually and collectively.

You don't have to try. I'm not asking you to try to be

enthusiastic about your life. I'm asking you to stop holding back, because I know you do. I see inside all of you, and your enthusiasm is growing and growing and growing. Dare to be uncool. Dare to jump on the bed in excitement for no reason at all. If on the inside you're saying that you don't feel that, haven't felt it in years, not since you were a little child, or that you don't even know what I'm talking about, remember—I'll be standing beside you with a little Cheshire grin, saying, *"Sure you don't... it's okay, it's okay."* You don't even have to figure out what it is inside of you that holds back on feeling excited. You've already tried that. Endlessly. You could probably list, in just a few seconds, at least five things that clamp down on your passion, enthusiasm, and sparkle for life.

> Keep asking yourself, "What am I choosing? What am I choosing today? What am I choosing now? Do I choose the miracle or do I choose boredom? Do I choose to just look good on the outside, or do I choose my own life? Please, stop choosing someone else's life. Choose yours. Say every morning, *"Today I choose my life. Today I am the miracle. Today I celebrate my unique existence."* As you say these things, feel the commitment. Feel yourself committing to miracles every day, all day.

If you're someone who doesn't normally jump up and down or shout from the rooftops in excitement, I'm not talking here about a complete personality overhaul. The sense of excitement comes from within and moves outward in your own way, not someone else's. Let it be unique unto you. But do take the time to let it be.

Yes, there is a lot of darkness in your world. Yes, there are a lot of difficulties. Do not allow that energy to be your guiding force. I promise you, I promise you—if there's an issue that you need to dig around in and figure out, if there's something you need to know, I'll help you. I'll put up a billboard. I'll take out some ads on the radio. I'll put that extra special book into your hand.

> All I'm asking is for you to pay attention and allow. If you do these two things—wake up and allow—you will not have to do it alone. You will not have to figure it all out. You will not have to come up with all the answers before you step forward. Do your best every day to let go of the destination, and recognize that the miracles are in the journey.

You will feel a sense of fulfillment and belonging when something is realized or has come to fruition, but as soon as it does, there'll be the next step.

> You are always in motion. You are always on the journey.

What I see so much of is how you hold yourselves back tightly, waiting for the destination to make itself known before you take the journey.

When you're on the journey, you can worry endlessly before you arrive at your destination. Like a child on a car trip asking, "*Are we there yet? Are we there yet? Are we there yet?*" While you're focusing on the question, everything is going by so fast that you're missing it.

Let your movement come more from within, and less from without. Live your own life, not the life of someone else. Others will influence and affect you, but don't let them move you unless you are being moved from within.

I would like you to write down some of the miracles in your life and share what you've written with another person. Think of the subtle miracles—the ones that give you faith. Something as subtle as thinking of a friend and they suddenly call. Use this daily. Also, write down what you're grateful for. These actions will awaken you to the miracles, both great and small, happening inside and all around you every day.

MEDITATION:

Sit quietly, and as you take deep breaths, I'd like for you to meditate a few moments on the miracles in your life, both great and small. As you breathe them in, open yourself to the excitement and the enthusiasm that they carry.

As you feel the miracles in your life, let yourself fill with gratitude. Move your mouth into a smile and while breathing in, feel how it shifts your energy, deepening and strengthening it.

Keep smiling at yourself. Smile at your life. Take 3 deep breaths and let go, let go, let go. Slowly open your eyes.

How wonderful to be in the presence of so many miracles. I thank you for allowing me to serve you. All I ask is that you share. Give back what you have been given, so that you may receive more.

Namaste ~

CHAPTER 18
Jesus on my toast

Before Mother came into my life I was unable to recognize a miracle. I read about them occurring and believed in their existence, but only from a distance. Like many people, I thought they were reserved for special occasions, like a wedding dress you only wear once in your life, even if you marry again. Who received miracles and who didn't, added to my *life is unfair* outlook.

Then there was what I, with my superior attitude, thought of as the *crazy* miracles. You know the ones I'm talking about—Jesus's image in toast, Mother Mary's in dirt on the side of a building, Elvis sightings, and of course, Bat Boy. I used to buy the *Weekly World News* and tape the most outrageous stories to my refrigerator. I was an ardent follower of Bat Boy. I believed, but not really.

Now I like everyday miracles, like waking up and being free from the obsession to eat until I pass out. These kinds of miracles feel more obtainable; less flashy.

I used to be afraid of big miracles, and was unable to recognize the small ones. If a big one happened to me, I thought I'd be overburdened by the obligation to somehow pay it back. But how do you pay back being the one to survive a disaster when others don't, or your cancer goes away, never to return, but your friend's doesn't? It always seemed to me that miracles came with a high interest rate that made repayment impossible. And if you didn't pay up, something bad would happen. It seemed safer to just let miracles happen to others.

After I awakened to Spirit, but before Mother, I learned

about synchronicity. Not the accidental coincidence kind, as defined in the dictionary, but the deliberate, *there is a plan* kind. It opened me to the possibility that there was a rhythm or flow that I was feeling, but not in control of.

I gradually became aware of greater forces at work around me, and sometimes through me. It was heady as well as humbling. I may only be as a grain of sand on the beach of humanity, but I was equal in possibility to all the other grains of sand. Finding the cure for cancer or becoming a famous celebrity may not have been on the list of my best possibilities, but I felt for the first time that I could create a life that worked for me, and that the forces that were swirling around me seemed to confirm their support through synchronicity. When I need to talk through something, someone will pick up the phone and be there for me. Or if I need to *stop* talking and go within, no one will answer. Once I opened my eyes and my heart, the everyday miracles were everywhere. Now they're not so small anymore. No matter what the support looks like, it's a big deal to me that I can recognize it and let it into my life.

Every day that I committed to abstaining from my food addiction, felt as though the universe was tripping over itself to help me. Some days the support was like a flood. It was as if I were destined to get well. When twenty-four hours passed and I hadn't binged or starved myself, I knew I was living in a miracle. After I strung more of those twenty-four hour periods together, I became the miracle.

After that, I saw and felt miracles everywhere. Nature was a powerful everyday miracle that could break through my fear and pain like nothing else. A friend told me that sometimes when she watches a program on television about the universe, about how vast it is, and the mind boggling events that had to have happened just right to make our planet inhabitable, she feels God so poignantly that she can barely hold it inside herself. I love that feeling of being lifted up and planted firmly on the earth. That's the miracle of life. Yes, of course, it's in the big things too, like waking up one day knowing that cancer is no longer ravaging your body. But don't overlook the small miracles. You never know when you'll find Jesus staring back at you from the toast on your plate.

It's in whatever holds our attention and lifts us up to be something greater than we were only moments before. Mother is helping me let go of my need to play it cool. She gives me permission to jump on the bed in excitement for the miracles I know in my bones to be in play now. She strums a cord inside me when She wants me to pay attention to events, in order to watch how they come together with intelligent synchronicity.

As a result, I want to take better care of the miracle that is my body, home to my being. Miracles inspire me to be more accepting and kind in my relationships, because the people in my life are just as miraculous as I am. I've also rediscovered the miracle that is our planet. It sustains us, supports our endeavors, and gives us a context and structure for our awakening.

What surprised me most, was feeling the immense gratitude for being granted a life. No matter what my parents did or didn't do, they gave me life. Mother has moved me from feeling burdened by that to celebrating it. Simple. Profound. A miracle.

CHAPTER 19
Doing what you love

In the previous chapters, you opened yourself up to consciously choosing love as the foundation of your life, and began taking actions to bring that about. This next teaching will focus on allowing and directing your inner Self to emerge and manifest out in the world. When you engage in an activity or event that you love, it feeds your life force and provides health benefits to your whole being. It's a strong choice to make on any given day. The strength of that choice creates its own vibration, and that vibration feeds the cells of your body with a lightness, strength, and vitality that expands through the whole of your life. This creates a sense of fulfillment, which comes with a life well lived. Even the smallest things in your life begin to take on a brighter and a lighter feeling.

Always, when you're in this state of being, your health is improved both physically and mentally. That's not to say that problems won't arise, or challenges won't happen. Bad days still come and still go. The larger feeling for you is a sense of dynamic living. When I say dynamic, I don't necessarily mean that it looks or sounds big, but that it feels big within you. Regardless of what it might look like to others, or even how it looks to *you* from the outside, what it feels like on the inside is big, spacious, and expanded. Every time you're doing what you love, you're making more room in your life; you're making more room inside. There's less clutter in your mind, less clutter in your heart, and as a result, less clutter in your body.

I'm going to address doing what you love, whether you

feel you already do what you love or not, or whether you're somewhere in between. You love some things, but not so much others. For now, doing what you love doesn't necessarily mean a career. It can lead to that, or to financial gain, but it's not necessarily the journey that your soul desires you to take. It will be unique for each of you. Does that mean you can't love what you do for a living? No, of course not.

This is about the discovery within of a particular feeling and vibration. It's doubtful that you will love everything that you do in your life, but it's also very common for humans not to do what they love, whether out of obligation or fear. Or maybe you once loved what you did, but somehow you're not loving it now. Things change, and I want to talk about how to keep up with those changes. You may love many things in the course of your life. What you loved ten or twenty years ago may not be what you love today—but given who you are as a human being, you have the capacity and ability to always be doing something you love.

Let me just talk about that statement, *"Doing what you love."* The kind of love I'm talking about is the love of self-fulfillment, which has a slightly different feel for most of you. In general, it's the feeling of looking forward to doing something. Even if it's challenging, you look forward to doing it. It's something that when you're doing it, you're very present. You're not bored, so you don't feel the need to let your mind drift, to think of other things, or to look for distractions. You tend to have very good focus.

It's also something that fulfills your ambition. Ambition is not a bad thing. For humans, it's the energy that makes you want to reach farther, stretch higher, know more, and meditate deeply. A sense of accomplishment is very important for human beings to feel on a regular basis. To

212

feel that you're contributing, not only to your own life, but to the lives of those around you, is what matters most. Whether in a small way, a big way, or something in-between, what's important is that you feel a sense of fulfillment when you're doing this thing; that there's no place you'd rather be. It's the gift that you not only give to yourself, but also feel was given to you. You feel fortunate to be able to do it. You feel lucky, as if the stars aligned and you were gifted with this thing.

Doing what you love can be as simple as reading a book or riding a bike. It might be your career, painting, singing, playing with a child, providing meals for the homeless, traveling all over the globe to meet new people and have new experiences, or staying close to home and digging in your garden.

There's an attitude held by many people, especially people in western society, that you must put everything else ahead of doing what you love; that somehow there isn't enough time, and other things take precedence. I would tell you to be very careful of that attitude.

> There should be something in your life, no matter how small, that fills you with a sense of fulfillment on a daily basis. If not, your physical, mental, and emotional health will suffer. Always.

It's surprising how you let other things become more important than doing what you love—even when doing what you love only takes a small amount of your focus. It's a feeling that you're not balancing the scales in your life. As a result, by the end of the day, you're often too tired to do anything but watch television or some other mindless thing, which doesn't give you a sense of fulfillment.

It's tiring to spend your day not doing what you love; very, very tiring. The lie that your body and mind will tell you is that you're too tired to do anything else that day, that you're done and just want mindless entertainment. This is the voice of fear. Doing what you love changes your life for the positive and that feeling builds on itself. Your health will improve as your thoughts become more and more positive. It has a very strong effect.

You can continue to do what you love in small increments. That's fine, but it's a very limited choice. There is indeed a way to build on this, so eventually you're spending the majority of the day doing what you love. When you love something, really love something, it lights you up. And I'm not talking about the kind of love you have for your favorite pizza or ice cream, I'm talking about what you feel passionate about, what excites you when you talk about it. The excitement can feel big or it can feel small, quiet, and deep. It doesn't matter how you feel it. You know when it's there. You know.

If you only let yourself do what you love in small increments or you're waiting to do what you love when you retire, look within to see what's holding you back. It's important for you to stop and illuminate your shadow to see why it's afraid to do what you love. Ask yourself if you're really willing to spend the whole of your days not doing something you're passionate about.

Ask what's more important; your life or maintaining your fear?

All of you have been given the extraordinary gift of life. Let go of thinking that you have to do something grand with that life. You're already doing something grand. You're living it; that's grand enough. Now move into doing what you love. Let's say you already do what you love or that you once did what you love, but you're not doing it now. Or maybe what you loved before, you're not feeling so excited about anymore. These are normal transitions. What I'm going to give you can be applied if you're already doing what you love and would like to do it more, or if you have absolutely no idea what it even is that you love. It's always a collection of different things that come together to create a feeling of fulfillment, of love. It's never just one thing, one focus, or one action. It's always a collection.

The first thing you'll discover when doing what you love is that somehow it includes all that's wonderful and unique about you. Whether it's your humor, adventurous Spirit, determination, love of people, or whatever else makes you *you*, it doesn't matter as long as you do what you love.

> What matters most is that you truly begin to identify your gifts. You may not even see them as gifts. Just notice what you're doing when you find yourself engaged in something.

What I mean by *engaged*, is when you feel connected to whatever you're doing, and when you do it, there's some kind of interest created. You'll know the difference when you're trying to be a part of something that you don't feel engaged with. You may feel very bored or detached, as though there's a space between you and whatever you're doing. You might enjoy it somewhat, you wouldn't say it was terrible or bad, but if someone were to ask if you'd like to do that again tomorrow, the answer would probably be *no*.

In turn, you also know what it feels like to be genuinely engaged. Whether it's in conversation with others or while doing an activity, as soon as you start doing it, you get lost in it. Time passes and you don't know where it's gone; what felt like thirty minutes to you was in actuality two hours.

It's a very good sign when you ask yourself,
"Where did the time go?"
Make a note of that.

It's easy not to see your talent for talking to people as a gift. You may take it for granted. When you talk to them, it's easy for you to think of things to say. You can interact with just about anyone. Not everyone has this particular gift, because they don't need it; if you have it, you do.

Other people may have commented that you're good at working with your hands, but to you it's just something that comes naturally.

Or maybe you have a way of seeing the bigger picture in such a way that it offers a new perspective to people who can't see it themselves. Or maybe you can see just one part of the picture, but to such a depth and degree that when part of a collaborative effort, it helps everyone piece together the picture as a whole.

Don't take anything that you do well for
granted. Write it down. Write down all the
activities that engage you, whether with or

without others. It doesn't necessarily need to be a happy engagement. Politics is a very heated subject for many of you, but for some of you, engaging in political discussions makes you feel alive and present. This ability is a gift. Don't focus on things that make you angry or enrage you. No. Excitement and passion don't necessarily bring happiness. Happiness is different than joy. Joy happens when you're engaged in a passionate pursuit. Whatever you love, whatever you enjoy, whatever engages you, whatever stimulates a passionate response within you, these are the things I'm encouraging you to write down and keep track of. This is very, very important.

Look back on things that you've done in the past and that you did for a while. Maybe circumstances changed and you never quite got back into things, but you remember what you used to enjoy, and what made you feel good within yourself. Write this down too. Take a chance. Combine some of these together.

Contemplate the things on your list. You may find that many are connected. See if a repetitive pattern begins to emerge. Your love of books and your ability to engage well with others may not mean that you want to become a writer, but it might mean that you're passionate about teaching others to read to help elevate literacy in your community.

Your interests can always be expanded into something wider, something bigger. If you used to love something but maybe not so much anymore, it's because it wants to evolve and you're not allowing it. Outwardly, it might feel like you don't want to teach people to read anymore. But instead of allowing that to move you in a different direction and to expand you in a different way, you just stop doing that one thing, without bringing anything in to replace it. Those same gifts will allow you to serve in a different manner. From the outside what's drawing you now might not seem to have anything to do with books or literacy, but somehow it has engaged the same passion and fulfillment within you.

> When something shifts in your life and you no longer get the same joy from it, there is work to be done; there are discoveries to be made, my beloved ones. Don't ever just leave something behind without creating something else to take its place. If you do, you'll risk leaving yourself disconnected from what you love, sometimes for years.

The surest way to keep yourself from doing what you love is, to let the grandiose mind get a hold of your passion. For example, a spiritual path can be tricky at times because when you touch divine bliss, you feel the extraordinary possibilities that exist, even if you only touch on those feelings occasionally. It's not a continuous knowing, but you've felt it, and its vast intricacies are wonderful to behold. Someone will tell me that they're very passionate about a certain something and that they *absolutely* want it for their own highest good and the highest good of everyone else too! They *insist* that they want to bring this particular thing to the world in an extraordinary manner to help shift the essence and vibration of humanity! But before you know it, the human self is cowering in the corner thinking, *Oh, no! Not me! I'm going to stay right here where it's safe and warm. I can't do that! It's way too big for someone like me!*

Don't do that to yourselves. Whether what you do changes the vibration of humanity is not up to you. So don't try to plan it. Don't let your ambitions dwell in the realm of fantasy. It's unhealthy and unwise. That's not to say that something you do in your life *won't* have a great impact on humanity, but you can't plan for it. It never works out that way.

What you *can* do is engage in your own life. And the way to engage is by doing what you love. There will still be challenges, there will be setbacks, some pain—but through it all, you'll have a sense of fulfillment knowing that you' re in the right place, at the right time, with the right people, doing the right thing, and that there's nowhere else you'd rather be.

You'll feel that you have everything you need, and for a time, you won't be thinking about getting more or doing something else. You're not planning ahead—you're just in it *now*—experiencing. If you stop for a moment to tune in, you'll realize you need nothing more in that moment. As a human adult, you'll always have responsibilities and commitments. But that shouldn't stand between you and doing what you love. Approach this without a label as an exercise in understanding your collective brilliance.

> *What are the things that you do well?*
> *Identify them. Then identify what you love*
> *doing. Just because you do something well,*
> *doesn't necessarily mean you love doing it.*

Within that gift or talent, you'll find something that connects you to what you love. Just because you're good with numbers doesn't mean you should become an accountant or mathematician. Don't assume that your gifts are automatically going to lead you in one direction. No. Being good at something isn't enough to fulfill you. It will give you satisfaction to a certain degree, but it will not bring true fulfillment.

What you're looking for is a *collection* of what you're good at. Then allow *that* to lead you to what you love. Maybe you already know what you love, but you're afraid to do it. You longingly stare at it and think that maybe tomorrow you'll finally begin. I want you to remember that you won't know if you love something until you allow yourself to try it. Recognize that you won't be attracted to doing something if the wonderful list of gifts inside of you didn't have the potential to arrange themselves in such a way as to bring it about. There's a connecting point between being good at something and doing what you love. When those two things come together, there's extraordinary fulfillment and a deep, deep sense of rightness.

When something you love ceases to feel fulfilling, don't abandon it completely as you take your gifts with you wherever you go. They'll simply translate into something new or different. It's also very important to keep yourself inspired when doing what you love. Indeed, some of you are earning or trying to earn a living doing what you love, or changing things so that at a later date you can do what inspires you. You'll want to spend more of your day doing what you love than what you don't, but the money may not come in very quickly. There may be a lot of feelings of procrastination. Be kind and patient with yourself, but always, always, you must seek to inspire yourself.

Who better to inspire you than yourself? You know what your gifts are. You're intimately acquainted with them, you know how they work and manifest. Remind yourself how good you are at the things you love, because it can be easy to get discouraged. If you're gardening for fun and because you love it and you're able to spend more time doing it, maybe you don't need to earn a living as a gardener.

Perhaps you're looking to change what you do for a living and you love to garden, but don't think you could actually earn enough money doing it to support yourself. What is it about you and gardening that come together to give you an extraordinary feeling? What does the garden offer? Which parts of you do you bring to it? What is it within the garden that calls to you? You must learn to pay attention to what you're doing and why you're doing it in order to help formulate what you love. Sometimes your fear is so great that you can't seem to establish, what you love doing no matter how hard you try. Chances are you'll have to spend time with that fear. You know that you keep yourself from doing what you love on a regular, continual basis due to the limitations and grandiosities you have set for yourself. Either way, you've set the conditions, therefore, they're almost impossible to achieve.

Try not to think about doing what you love in terms of work, money, or by labeling it as just a hobby. Don't. Do take a chance on yourself. Take a chance on trying something new. Take a chance on bringing something back into your life that you once did and loved, but that for some reason you stopped doing. You don't even need to know why.

You can wait to do what you love. Or you can do what you love now. Fear can be a very powerful barrier. Often, you may not even be able to understand your fear, or even identify it. Fear can be so elusive that you may think you aren't afraid to go out and do your thing, but you also notice that something keeps preventing you, day after day after day after day. You don't pick up the paintbrush. You don't go out in the garden, go up in a hot air balloon, get on a bicycle, or contact the literacy society. There's a strange, nebulous, invisible force that keeps you rooted in place. Not going backward, but not really going forward either; just sort of moving sideways.

These barriers require work and effort to move through. You have to take down your own walls.

Write down what you're good at, what you know you excel in, no matter how small, no matter what area it's in, no matter how it applies, and focus on it. Don't just listen to these words and think to yourself, *Yes, that feels like a lot of truth; I understand what Mother is saying.* You must actually do the work. Take the action. Write down your gifts. Remind yourself often what you're good at. Don't assume to know what it might turn into, or how it might coalesce to create a certain something for you to do. Just start with your talents, and each day go within and feel yourself open to a willingness to allow your gifts to formulate in such a way that your path is illuminated. It's not that you don't know what to do or what you love. That's not true. You know it's already within you. You just have to look for it because it's behind the walls.

Maybe your fears and barriers are small, so you allow yourself to garden on the weekends, but during the week you only do "responsible" things. Instead of reserving the gifts that take you into the garden for weekends only, allow the garden to whisper in your ear as to how you might do this the majority of your time rather than just a few days a week. It's not that you don't know how; it's that you're *unwilling* to *reveal* to yourself how because you're not ready to know. So how do you get ready? You highlight your gifts, what you're good at, what you excel at. Even if your talents seem completely unrelated, it doesn't matter—put them all down on paper. Take that paper to a quiet place and feel for the gifts inside you. Your ability to commune with others, your love of the earth, your fascination with flowers, your sense of humor, your ability to clean a house until it sparkles, your joy with your children, the great love you have for your cats...

Now, bring them all together. Allow your gifts to transform the barriers that keep you from knowing and doing what you love to do. Allow them to help you transform something you used to love but aren't feeling so much anymore, into something extraordinary. They're only mental walls you've constructed inside, not a lack of knowing. You don't have to go out there to find what you love doing. It's already inside you.

As you imagine each of the gifts within you, they'll come together like puzzle pieces, a little at a time. Begin to transform your barriers and start illuminating your fear. See the walls, the fears, as nothing but paper dragons waiting for you to simply acknowledge them. While your barriers have presence and do affect your life, the only power they actually have is the power you give them. If you're willing to let your gifts illuminate the wall, you'll see it for what it is, and realize it has no real hold on you. It's not controlling your life or keeping you from happiness. No one or thing is keeping you from doing what you love. It's simply your lack of willingness to discover what that is. It's understandable. Each of you has a variety of reasons as to why you're unwilling, and they're all valid.

> *If you feel that you're at a place in your life*
> *where on a regular, daily, on-going basis*
> *you want to do more of what you love,*
> *begin to place your focus on your gifts.*
> *When you focus on your talents, they come*
> *together and collaborate to help show you*
> *the way. Engage that fantastic mind of*
> *yours. Take a look at the interesting picture*
> *that's forming there. Ask how you can*
> *bring it forth. Celebrate what seems to be*
> *coming forward, and ask how you can best*
> *act on it.*

Listen closely to yourself. I've heard you describe exciting feelings and interests emerging from you, and then in the same breath, say, *"But I don't know what any of it means. I don't know what I want or what I love to do."* Yet you will have just moments before described the wonderful things that are holding your interest and that you're passionate about, and all the experiences you're having. But because you want to skip right to the end and know how it's all going to turn out, you risk missing out on the good things happening in the meantime.

> Doing what you love is about being
> committed to yourself, because you know
> your life is the greatest gift that you'll ever
> receive. In essence, it's the only thing you
> really *ever* have, this life of yours. The
> harder you try to find what you love from
> the outside in, the farther from it you'll find
> yourself.

Once you find the life within, only *then* will it manifest on the outside. You're always given many different ways in which to do what you love, even if in the beginning you don't feel you're good at it. For example, let's say you discover that what you really love is music, and you've always wanted to play an instrument. When you first start playing an instrument, you may not sound so good. But when you're holding that instrument and feeling the possibilities, the fact that you're making music at all, even if it doesn't sound very good, brings you a sense of fulfillment. And you understand that just because you're not good at music in the beginning, all your gifts together are designed to make you quite good with enough practice. It might take you many years of study to get there, but you won't mind because you love it. You've finally let yourself do what you love.

Will you ever make money at it? Who knows? Maybe yes. Maybe no. The fact that you've allowed yourself to do it is gift enough; not only for you, but also for all those in your life. It means your health is strong and you're happy. This often happens with young people; they'll explore their talents and abilities even if they have to do another job to support their dreams.

Don't think in terms of dreams fulfilled or
unfulfilled just because you think you have
to find a way to earn money so that you can
do what you love more often. Don't try to
figure it out. Just commit to doing what you
love. Commit, no matter what, to feeling all
the gifts that you've been given. Each of
your gifts allow you to expand on them so
they can become greater, or go in a
different direction in order to bring about a
particular result. Your gifts are not static.
They come from vibrational qualities
within you that have the ability to change
and shift depending on what you ask of
them.
Give yourself over to the idea of doing what
you love. Start doing one thing, and then
build on it.

You have the capacity to love a lot of different things,
and to do a lot of different things in life. For most of you,
there's that one special thing that when it comes together
right, is a wonderful expression of Self. It's an active,
energetic, emotional, physical, and mental expression of
Self. That one thing might show itself in different ways with
different groups and individuals for a while. But when you
bring these parts of your Self together and turn them into
action, doing that thing you love will be at the core of
everything you do in life.

Know that you're not static and if you've taken on
something that feels large, like a career, and you're getting
bored with it or you don't think you like it anymore, don't
quit right away.

*Look at the different aspects of your gifts.
Everything you do has different parts to it.
Look at each of them individually and
make sure that it's not just a few that are
influencing your boredom with the whole.
Sometimes you can shift or let go of some
parts and bring in new ones. Then, all of a
sudden, you love doing it again, and once
more it inspires, fulfills, and excites you.*

Regardless of where you're led or what you fall into doing, the deeper need is to allow yourself to do what you love.

*Take a chance. Find what you love and do
it. Take a chance and do more of what you
love. Take a chance by going more deeply
into what you love.*

MEDITATION:

Sit quietly and close your eyes. Take several deep breaths. Settle into your own being... the center of yourself. Feel your awareness of Self. Feel the presence within your body.

Allow yourself to focus on three of your gifts. As you look at each one, just notice how they feel from within, and how it feels to know that you have these gifts.

Somewhere inside of you is the knowing of what you love to do. Allow your three gifts to move towards, to connect with, and to find what you love. If you come up against a barrier that feels like blank space when you try to focus on what you love, or if you feel nothing at all, allow your three gifts to break through and saturate that nothing, that barrier.

Feel the desire your gifts have to connect you with what you love, to formulate into what you love, and to illuminate the path to doing what you love. This is what your gifts were made for. It's why you have them. They want to expand. They want to create.

Your gifts are integral to helping you discover the vehicle and means for doing what you love. Commit yourself to knowing, to finding, to discovering, and to allowing yourself to do what you love. It's all there within you.

Now let go of the focus on your gifts, your barriers, and the doing of what you love. Just settle into whatever there is to feel within, in this moment.

Now take three deep breaths and on the exhalation, let go of the meditation.

You may slowly open your eyes.

Doing what you love may not feel easy, but that's only because of the walls you've built within you. When you bring your gifts forward, things become simple, and very doable; challenging maybe, but hard, no.

What's really hard is not doing what you love. What's hard is maintaining the barriers, so that what you love can stay hidden. What's hard is making things too grandiose or too complicated. Simplify. Break it down. Celebrate your gifts every day. They will lead you where you want to go.

I thank you for allowing me to serve you. Be kind to yourself and to each other and know that I love you.

Namaste ~

CHAPTER 20
Send in procrastination

I'm fortunate that I love channeling Mother Mary. The ability She gave me to do this work is both a challenge and a joy. It's like I imagine climbing a mountain would be—enormous effort and incredible fulfillment. Yet I also have a deep need to be creative, and at this point in my life, I love to write.

When I call and ask my girlfriend, who's a writer, how she's doing, she says she's doing well because she's writing this week. Doing what you love is a difficult teaching for me to write about, because on one hand, like my friend, I'm doing what I love as I write these words; but on the other hand, I've been trying to finish a book for ten years. The first five years, I was content to take classes and try new things, but without thinking too much about doing anything with it. I felt happy just writing for myself. Then my creations took on an energy of their own and wanted to be shared. I didn't want to change the world, nor was it a consuming ambition, but it needed a public outlet just the same. I had gotten good feedback and felt I could pull off an actual book at some point.

As soon as I began to focus on publication, like an infestation of chipmunks in my garden, my doubts punched holes in the foundation I had built with my writing. I felt off balance and lacking in confidence. So my ever-faithful sidekick—procrastination—came to my rescue and assured me that I could wait until Monday to write. But... Monday never came. I began to go six months at a time with only enough written words to fill a comment card at a restaurant coming out of me.

I'm not entirely sure why I feel the need to publish my work. Maybe I do have a strong inner drive to do so that's been buried alive under a mountain of doubt and self-loathing. As I come to accept and love myself, I sift through the rubble and find aspects of myself that I had no idea existed.

Here's the kicker—I want to write fiction. I enjoy crafting memoir, but don't want to do that exclusively. Memoir makes me feel like I'm opening an intimate dialogue with my reader. This book is a sharing of my devotional experience with Mother, the strength She has given me, and the tangible difference She has brought about in my life, but oddly enough, I don't aspire solely to be a devotional/inspirational author.

But I haven't allowed myself to write and complete a novel yet. I feel some shame around that. Doing what I love has to feel safe for me. If I take the risk to expose my life and my abilities to a wider audience, I feel as though my writing ability should be fully formed, perfected, before you read this. There will be some who don't like what I'm offering, and for a time, that was enough to scare me off.

If I am still long enough, Mother helps me find the solution. With gentle strength, She said, *"Start here, Beloved,"* and helped me create the structure for this book. It began when two women devoted to Mother's teachings volunteered their efforts to transcribe Mother's audio into written documents. As I began reading what they sent to me, I was amazed at how well it transitioned from the spoken word to the written word. The more I read, the more an obvious structure began to emerge. I spoke to friends about the possibility of putting it together into book form, and the response was a resounding *yes!*

Because I'm a full-body channel, all Her teachings are

spoken, so I never thought a book was possible. It had to be shown to me that it was. Mother made it feel obvious in the beginning because She knows I don't do well with subtleties, especially when there's a high risk of exposure. Mother told me which teachings to use and the order She wanted them in. She made it very clear that She wanted me to write these short, companion memoir pieces. I decided to put them at the end.

"Send in the procrastination!" my fear shouted. Mother knew, oh, great deity that She is, that if each chapter I wrote was only a few pages, and my writing came at the end, I would be willing to do it. In my mind, that meant people could skip my part if they chose, since they would have already gotten the good stuff at the beginning of the book.

Later with the help of a good friend, who is a successful author, I came around to her idea of putting a memoir piece after each of Mother's teachings. I could feel the buoyancy of that, even as my knees were shaking. It was this kind of support that would empower me to take the next step.

Since there was only one woman I knew who was devoted to Mother and was also a writer and editor by profession, it was again made obvious who should edit the book. Because really, what other editor could you tell that you can't make many changes, and Mother will only do rewrites through you? It had to be someone who knew Her voice and had a strong relationship to Her without me. My editor has not only been a great editor of Mother's words, but also a tireless supporter of my finishing this in order to offer it to others.

Mother provides not only the obvious necessities, like the money to pay for it, but the support I need to keep moving forward. People who know what I'm attempting ask me how it's going and express their desire to read it the moment it's available. That gives me the confidence that more than five people will want to read it.

I have to show up for what I love in order to be given the opportunity to do what I love. I can't create the opportunities on my own; I can only open myself up to receive them. I have to commit to sitting down in this chair and putting words on a page and the only way I can do that is with Mother's support.

It seems strange that doing what I love would take such an effort. If I love it, why doesn't it come more easily? Because, for me to do what I love, I have to accept the gifts I have inside of me, be willing to use them, and celebrate them with a party everyone is invited to attend. *Not easy.* (But, if you're reading this in a published form, you'll know it got a little easier.)

There's a knowing inside of me that tells me if I can go through the process of finishing, publishing, and offering this book to the public, it will be easier for me to show up and write a novel. This is how Mother provided the path for me to go deeper into doing what I love. She gives me constant support and minute shifts in my perception of what's safe for me. My procrastination is there if I need it, just like the old stuffed purple rabbit I used to think would slay my dragons for me. That belief is still active some days, but now it sits on the shelf more often than not.

I was told six weeks after my son was born that I would be doing a lot of writing in my fifties. I was thirty-nine when a numerologist, whose table I sat down at for fifteen minutes at a Body, Mind, and Spirit festival, gave me that information. Today as I write this, I'm forty-nine, and it looks like I'm right on track.

Support is always there if I ask for it, and sometimes it's even there when I don't. If I want to consistently do what I love, I have to ask for that support. I have to reach out and ask for what I need. I don't always get it directly from the first person I ask, but it will come from someone if I just keep asking. It reminds me that my needs are worth fulfilling. Every time I'm willing to receive support, my procrastination stays on the shelf another day.

Doing what I love also gives me the courage to support and love others with less judgment and more freedom. Like all the teachings in this book, I'm still navigating this one. The path is bumpy, but smoothing out with every word.

CHAPTER 21
Commitment

Breathe in your choice to be here now, and feel the trust in yourself growing. Know that you are here to receive. Breathe and open yourself up. Open your mind, your heart, your Spirit. Settle in so that you can fully integrate and truly feel what is being offered to you as you read these words.

Understanding commitment can help you to expand and deepen your relationship, not only to the essence of yourself, but also to the whole of your life. Being born into the body is a commitment; the very greatest commitment that you will make in this life.

Commitment is to decide, on a very deep level, that you will bind yourself in communion and relationship to something or someone.

When I say bind, I'm not necessarily implying a permanent state of being. You can bind yourself to something or someone, and later find yourself coming to completion and moving on to other commitments, but the energy or essence of the original commitment that you made will stay with you throughout your whole life.

Your life, in many ways, is a series of commitments, and commitment goes beyond choice. A choice is something that opens a doorway and introduces you to an action. It gives you the opportunity to decide that you want to try something. Commitment takes choice to a much deeper level.

When you were a child, your choices, and then your commitments, were often guided by your parents or those who raised you, by your environment, and by society. School is a wonderful example of this. It may not have been your idea to go to school, but you chose originally to come into a life where school was a part of it. You decided that, through your parents, you would make this choice and commit to school for however long your society decided that you needed to go. But as you age and mature, you don't require your parents to encourage your choices. You learn to make your own. You learn what it means to choose, to have the gift of choice, and also what it means to live with the consequences of those choices.

Commitment comes from a decision deep within Self to align with a certain someone, group, cause, or vocation. It's an action that you do repeatedly because you enjoy the results that you get. Commitment is not something you're unfamiliar with. No matter who you are in the world, you're living with commitment just by staying in your body. A part of your Soul committed to living, to animating the physical body so that you could experience life. Your parents committed to each other, even if it was only long enough to come together once to create you. That was a commitment on the deepest level. No matter how it might look in the human world, energetically, it's a commitment.

You're in the process of engaging in commitments now, which are preparing you for the commitments yet to come. Occasionally, you want or need something for your happiness and fulfillment, and find it very challenging to commit to whatever or whomever it would take to help you bring this thing, whatever it is, into fruition.

Most often, what you struggle with committing to most is a deeper sense of Self, and the recognition that you're a deeply capable and wise individual. What you are able to create in any given lifetime is practically limitless.

It's easy to take for granted the little things that you do every day. Maybe you're very good at making others feel comfortable and welcomed, and you always have a ready smile for people. Maybe you have a gift for healing, whether it be through your hands, voice, or just your intelligence and ability to communicate well. Whatever your gifts are, whatever you bring to your life, there's a tendency to take all these little things that you do each day for granted. The truth is, all those seemingly small things are a constant reminder of how powerful you really are. You can do something as simple as shifting the way you eat by adding something healthy to your diet, and that small adjustment can make an enormous difference on your physical and mental health, your outlook on life, and even your happiness.

Once you commit to not eating that certain thing anymore, there's a tendency to just brush it aside as if it were the easiest thing in the world for you to do. You often miss the impact, the importance, of what you've done for yourself or others. I'm not speaking of importance in a way that suggests you're superior to others so that you can think yourself better than. No. This is about understanding how truly powerful you are, and how much it took for you to stop your poor eating habits in order to have more health and vitality.

Your life is made up of thousands and thousands of little choices, and some of them will lead to commitments. Those commitments, in essence, help you to understand more deeply what's important to you.

> *Are you committed to eating poorly, or are you committed to eating well and in a healthy manner? Are you committed to love, or are you committed to fear? Are you committed to a vibrant life, or are you committed to depression? For each of you, it will be a mixture of all of these things, of course, but your commitments will honor how you apply your energy. You can be just as committed to unhappiness as you are to happiness.*

There is a great power in commitment. Often your commitments can be unconscious, because consciously, most of you would not want to commit to unhappiness. If it's something that keeps happening day in and day out, it's meant to help you begin to understand what you're committed to that you may be unaware of.

If you're committed to your children, it manifests by you consistently showing up for them and being there for them to the best of your ability. If you're committed to your work, it's apparent because you continue doing the work. Does the way you're committing bring you happiness? Sometimes it's not enough to commit to a particular thing and just believe that it's going to bring you happiness. This is often where people who are on a spiritual path become confused and have a difficult time finding peace or joy.

Others may be able to commit to something outside of themselves, and it creates a deeper happiness within. Some of you may be able to do that very easily. Often what happens when you choose a conscious life, living from the inside out rather than the outside in, all of a sudden things are very different. What happens easily for others may not happen easily for you.

> *I want you to give some thought and consideration to the internal things that you are committed to.*

Recognize that it's your commitment to your internal life that will give you a much easier road to committing to things outside of yourself—career, finances, people. Regardless of what your relationship is to those things, it's easier to commit when you're internally committed.

What does that mean? It means you're dedicated deeply within yourself to your own happiness, peace of mind, and willingness to let go of suffering. You must acknowledge that being on this spiritual path is exactly what you've committed to. You have committed to your own inner life; an inner life that awakens each and every day more and more powerfully to bring you greater consciousness, to allow you to serve others, but more importantly, to find your own inner peace. I say more importantly because it's very hard to serve others when you're not at peace within yourself. It's very hard to feel that you're not being put upon, asked too much of, pulled in too many directions, or overwhelmed.

> *Committing to yourself, is to be in alignment with yourself.*

What are some of the things that might challenge your commitment? The biggest one that I see with human beings is that you don't believe in your own worth and power. If someone you loved struggled with over-eating a certain food but after years of trying to find balance, they were finally able to let it go, and as a result they felt much better, your reaction would be to praise them.

You would probably be impressed, especially if it were something like sugar, which is so pervasive in your culture. You might say to them, "My goodness! It's amazing that you were able to abstain and now it's been six months! How incredible! But if you were the one doing it, you might feel in the beginning a sense of accomplishment and some pride in yourself, that you were finally able to let go of this thing and to live your life without it, not missing it, needing it, or using it to punish yourself. There may be a short period when you feel that you've done well, but what *I've* noticed with humans is that your initial positive feelings are quickly gone.

When you can't feel your own worth, you cannot connect with your own power. I don't mean the energy to do something, heal someone, or create something outside of yourself, but your own authentic *power*. The life force that courses through your body *is* your *real* power. When you can't feel that, it's hard to stay in the knowing that you can choose healthy foods, that you can exercise on a regular basis, or commit to anything else you feel you need in your life.

You have the ability to give yourself gift after gift after gift. Why are you worth it? You're worth it simply because you *are*—because you *exist*. No matter what you've done or haven't done, or said or haven't said up to this moment, you're still worth all the gifts that you will allow yourself to have; and you can't have too many gifts! This is not like Christmas, and God is not Santa Claus. There's an unlimited supply of energy and love available for your use, in order to make the adjustments you wish for so much easier.

To eat more or less of something is not so much a commitment to eating or not eating, but a commitment to Self. It's the deep desire to be a part of something because it brings you fulfillment and uplifts you. It might also be very painful, but through the pain you're shown a part of yourself you never thought you'd find, a part that's full of courage, commitment, and stick-to-itness, no matter what. Then you come out on the other side, and you're amazed at what you've become and how deeply you've delved into Self.

Once you step on this path, you start to realize that there's really only one commitment; the commitment to Self. That commitment goes in so many different directions, but when those directions stop feeding you, when you feel a commitment to someone or something hasn't brought you what you had hoped for, first and always, find the commitment to yourself.

Part of a spiritual life and practice is recommitting to Self every day. One of the best ways you can do that is to marvel at the fact that you're alive. Even though you know there are no coincidences, look with awe at all the things that had to come into alignment just so your parents could bring you forth. Regardless of how that came to be, you've been given the gift of life, and that gift is a deep commitment to all else that lives within and around you. Begin your day by marveling at your life and the smallest things it contains and go from there. Feel committed to yourself.

Understand what that means and how it
feels to you. Commitment is a choice that
you make again and again.

When you commit to a marriage, you commit to show up in that relationship every day. What about your marriage and relationship to yourself? Many of you are extraordinary at allowing gifts to come to you. You're taking better care of your mental and physical health than you ever have. But some of you are still struggling deeply, however, because you refuse to acknowledge your self-worth.

I understand that you may have grown up with messages that said you weren't worth very much. You can choose to commit to that appraisal, to the voices that first made you feel unworthy. Or you can discover that there's an easier way by committing, deeply and utterly, to your own self-worth.

Some of you have children, or possibly a younger sibling, and were tasked with protecting them, being present for them, and watching out for them. Through that, you began to see how important life is, and that you are also worth protecting, being looked out for, and taken care of.

Maybe others didn't look out for you very well. That wasn't your fault and has nothing to do with your worth. That was their choice, based on their understanding of commitment. You have your own. You are your own person. You have your own worth. When you commit to yourself, you begin to dedicate your life to *you.* This isn't about being selfish or self-centered. It's about committing; to dedicating yourself in such a way that it opens everything within you up so that it's easier for your commitment to Self to move in new directions; you'll have better relationships with everyone in your life as you begin to take better care of

Self. What can be rewarding is allowing yourself to commit to endeavors or actions that create happiness in your life; to learn and create something new and bring to fruition that which rests in your heart.

> Over the next few days and weeks, I want
> you to think about what commitment
> means to you. Remember, what I'm
> encouraging you to look at are your
> priorities concerning your commitments.
> You'll know it's important when you feel an
> energy that says, *"Yes, I'm going to align*
> *myself with..."* a thing, action, or person.
> Within that alignment, you are given the
> opportunity to discover yourself more
> intimately. But when you're not aware of
> your commitments to Self and how they
> move out from within you, it's easy to think
> that things are being done *to* you, rather
> than realizing that what's happening is a
> reflection of what you're committed to.
> Open your mind and commit to your own
> self-worth, and marvel at your life.

What does it mean when you commit? It means that you've decided you're going to stick with it, no matter what, until you're told or shown otherwise. You're going to show up and you're going to do what is asked of you, whether it's a career, children, a significant other, pets, even your plants. When you consciously keep your commitments alive, something inside of you shifts. You make a deeper choice.

If you don't review your commitments, they can

become habits that no longer serve you. Don't forget the power of your commitments; they are there to show you your priorities. Commitments should not be entered into lightly. That's why you may have a long time between lives, because your Spirit remembers it all.

All that I'm asking you to do in the next days and weeks is to explore the commitment to your life. It's not easy. It may even feel odd, but don't take your life for granted. Even if it's hard or you're in pain right now—*please* don't take your life for granted. Don't take your *commitment* to your life for granted—because what you are capable of is *extraordinary*. Your self-worth cannot be quantified. It is much, much too great for that. If you don't feel it, it's because at some point you chose to commit to being unworthy.

Take some time. I always encourage you to write about these things. It would be lovely if you incorporated journaling into your spiritual practice, so that when I ask you to write about something it can just be part of the journaling process. Writing offers a gift of revelation that often doesn't occur when you just think about something. Write about your commitment to yourself. How does that feel to you? Do you feel it at all? Can you even conceptualize what I'm talking about? Do you feel that it takes a commitment to have the Soul reside within

> the body, for the body to grow and mature, to live a life? Does this resonate with you in any way?
> Find the commitment if it's there for you. Feel if you can, just for a little bit, the commitment to yourself. Can you start your day by committing to your own life? Again, this means to dedicate, align, and show up for yourself—every day, every week, every month, every year. Show up and be present to and accept your worthiness and your power. You may not know all you can create or bring to life, but let go of the need to know until you can acknowledge it.

Don't *think* you have worth; know and commit to it. Accept it as real because when you know that you're worth all the gifts waiting for you to receive them, then it's easy to eat more of one thing and not another. It's easy to exercise, because you're worth it. You are worthy of a healthy body, a clear mind, a balanced life, and to be free of pain.

I'll tell you a little something about how humans work inside. Think about this as you explore commitment. If you perceive that you've made mistakes and missed opportunities, that somehow you've created a life of lack for yourself, done terrible things to others and your Self, you may think that before forgiveness takes place you must pay penance. Do you know what *penance* means? *Punishment for yourself.* That somehow you deserve to pay for what you've done or what you didn't do.

Sometimes in life, you're more dedicated or
committed to your punishment, to serving
out your penance, however long or
whatever that entails, before you allow
yourself happiness.

If you commit each day, to your unquestioned worth, your happiness, and feel that commitment extending out, and infusing all your other commitments, then you would find a deeper clarity in understanding your priorities. You would recognize what you've placed importance on that does not serve you, and how you can enhance what you feel *is* important and that *does* serve you.

When you are served this way, through people, your actions, and your endeavors in life, then you serve. It's automatic. It feels good to serve. It feels right to serve; it feels normal to serve because you're not so worried about gathering certain things to you to create worth.

When you come from a commitment to
your own sense of value, then you don't
waste any more time trying to find or
create your worth.

When you can acknowledge that your worth already exists, and you can accept, commit, and dedicate yourself to that acceptance, there is more ease. You don't have to continue your penance. You don't have to continue your punishment. It really is fairly simple. It may not feel easy to you, but it's fairly simple to shift your focus and commit to your happiness, worth, power, and life, and to feel yourself step into that dedication and alignment.

You can't know what the power and worth in your life will create. You don't know what it will bring to you. Find your worth now. Know it. Never allow anyone to tell you that you are unworthy. Whatever anyone tried to convince you of in the past, whether it was intentional or not, it's over. It's past.

> Today, you're worthy of commitment to Self and the deep, abiding energy that says yes to life, yes to whatever makes you feel better, yes to taking care of yourself in such a way that you're vibrant, full of life, and full of energy. Whatever that takes, this is what you invest your time and energy in and what you focus on. *This* is what you commit to.

When you do, all flows out from there, and the people in your life get enough of you and you get enough of them. The endeavors in your life bring to you enough because you bring enough to them. There is *no* lack. It's only your mind that thinks there's not enough, and when you think there's lack out there, it's because you haven't taken the time to find the abundance inside of yourself. It truly is that simple. Let it be simple today.

MEDITATION:

Sit quietly and close your eyes.

Take deep breaths into your body. At first, just allow yourself to feel your body. Feel the energy flowing through you from head to toe. Feel the air and the light upon your skin. Feel your presence, here and now.

Now feel your Spirit surrounding you, holding you—part of your body, your Soul. You are one being with a mind, body, and Spirit. This is life that you're feeling—your life—your spirit, mind, and body are your life.

If you're in your body now, alive within your body, you are committed to your life. For however long it lasts, you're committed to your life. Feel that commitment by your very presence.

Deep within yourself, using intention as your focus, using all your awareness and presence, commit to your worth. Allow yourself to feel the infinite value of your life force as it moves through your body, animating it with life, with thought, with feeling, with emotion, with movement, with love. All these things come to you through this commitment to life you've made. That commitment, your life, is worth more than *anything* outside of you. It's equal in worth to all the beings, physical and non-physical, that fill your world.

Now, with that same deep focus and intention, commit to your own happiness. Know that your Soul knows exactly how to help you create that. All that is required is your commitment. Know what your worth is, that there is so much happiness for you, and that your own happiness would never come at the cost of another's. There's so much, so much.

Commit now, dedicate, and align yourself to your happiness.

Feel the power of commitment; it goes far beyond choice. It's a deep alignment of the beliefs within your Soul, within your higher consciousness, within the joy of life that is inherent within you. Feel your energy align.

Through the power of your commitment, through your own happiness, you will bring happiness to others. You will enlighten them, awaken them, and serve them.

Never forget how extraordinary each element of your growth, your expansion is. Every time you're able to do something that yesterday you were unable to do, rejoice!

Remember. Acknowledge your power your deep commitment, and all that it took to create the movement, to create the shift, to bring forth and allow yourself to receive the gift.

Now take three deep breaths and on the exhalation, let go of the meditation. Keep with you your self-worth, your happiness, and your commitment to your life. Never forget, always remember.

On the last exhalation, go to your knees and place your forehead on the floor and relax into child's pose, grounding your energy deep into Mother Earth. Know that she's here to support you and to sustain you, to help you live your commitment to life.

Wonderful. You may slowly sit up and open your eyes.

I thank you for allowing me to serve you. Rejoice in your commitment to Self, beloved ones. It's where all your love flows from. It's my great hope that you can allow more happiness into your life each and every day, as you acknowledge your commitment to yourself. If you cannot remember your worth on any given day, remember my voice, my words, and my presence, so that you will know and remember the power of yours.

Namaste ~

CHAPTER 22
An ocean in a thimble

When I was in my twenties and my relationships with men didn't work out, I loved to tell anyone who would listen that men were commitment phobic. Turns out, it was *me*. I lived my life believing the grass was greener everywhere except where I was standing. Serenity and contentment were as far away as the moon. An urgent voice inside would tell me to move on. Putting down roots risked me being bound to others. The ever-present weight of my unreasonable expectations for my partners made the dynamic in my relationships dysfunctional. I wanted them to read my mind and make my dreams come true. It was the age-old Cinderella story. What happens after the ball is over and you settle into everyday life? I was clueless, and that made almost everything they did intolerable because I wanted them to have the answers, but they were just as lost as I was.

My inability to commit represented my fear of life. On some level I knew that if I committed to something, change would happen. I wanted to know ahead of time what those changes would be before I was willing to commit. If I committed to my acting career I might start getting parts, and then people would expect things of me that my shadow had convinced me I could never fulfill. Things as simple as showing up for rehearsals on time and knowing my lines seemed out of reach.

I had and still have to some degree a profound fear of disappointing people. I craved love and approval, yet felt I could never measure up. I still feel this in my romantic relationships. Committing to be naked with someone, physically and emotionally, was to be avoided like a shark feeding frenzy. Now I crave the intimacy commitment brings, but often don't know how to find my way in.

When I hit bottom with my eating disorder and found help, I understood that if I didn't commit to my recovery, I would die. I chose life, but kicked and screamed for the first five years because it involved a mountain of commitment. I couldn't stay out of the food without being committed to following a structure and staying close to Mother. Some days I despised what I saw as my weakness to such an extent that I wanted to do violence to myself and the people I was close to. I wanted to tear everyone down and make them feel small so they could huddle in the dark with me.

Grace carried me until I could crawl, and now, for twenty-two years, I have stuck with my recovery. It's my longest held commitment to date. Being committed to myself helped restore my self-confidence and love of life.

At first, I didn't recognize what I was doing to get well and recover as a commitment. I was just surviving from one meal to the next and trying to introduce a little life in between. I had to fill the space with something. I was encouraged to fill it with things that made me feel like a toddler surrounded by her village.

My friends and I spent Saturday nights sitting in a circle on the green and gold shag carpet in a friend's living room, dressed in sweat pants, and pouring our hearts out. Instead of a drink in our hands, we held tissue. Instead of talking over the raucous noise in a bar, we began to listen. Like the sunrise each morning, help was given to me. I didn't take it much of the time (especially in the beginning) but like my shadow on a sunny day, if I looked for help, it was always there.

My second longest commitment has been to Mother. I could not have done the second without the first. I have to keep them in that order because I can't keep my commitment to Mother if I'm consumed with obsession and destructive living.

I was living in Sedona when Mother first came to me. Up to that point I had been channeling smaller energies, nature spirits and extraterrestrials. My roommate at the time was a powerful energy worker and had an unquenchable need for information. He wanted me to start channeling Mother Mary. He felt we would be a good fit.

I knew his ambitions far outstripped mine, so I didn't think anything would come of it. About two weeks after he'd brought it up, I was in a deep meditation. I had the ability to feel my body dissolve and become one with the Spirit realm. It was here that Mother Mary first came to me like a warm breeze on a perfect spring day. She wrapped me up and held me in my first visceral experience of unconditional love. *"Beloved,"* She whispered, and from then on I was Hers. She was the sun that rose in my heart and filled it with hope and the knowing that She had always held me with exquisite care in Her hands, and She always would.

The image She projected in my mind was of a feminine form draped in robes of blue and green, with only the suggestion of a face surrounded by the vastness of creation. Years later, She validated my experience when I went to the gallery opening of my artist friend, Katharine Dahl. Two years before, Mother had requested that Katharine paint a portrait of Her while Katharine was blindfolded. It took Katherine awhile before she was able to commit to the request. The result was extraordinary. I stood before it as it hung on the wall of the art gallery and almost collapsed to my knees. The painting was almost an exact re-creation of my first vision of Her come to life. The power emanating from it swept through me, and I suddenly felt that the impossible just became possible. Katharine named the painting, *Green Mary*. Simple. Perfect. This is only one of the thousands of ways Mother has validated our commitment to each other. And I've needed every one.

Mother explained to me that She and I had an agreement in this life for me to channel Her. And then She did the most unexpected thing—She asked *me* if *I* wanted to honor that agreement. I had never felt so empowered in my life. What astonished me most was that I knew in my bones that if I said *no*, Her love for me wouldn't diminish.

Yes, shot through my consciousness like lava from an erupting volcano, burning every one of my doubts in its path before they could form. I had never wanted anything so much in my life. The rightness inherent in my agreement still resonates today.

As soon as the giddy feeling of first contact and my roommate's smirking satisfaction had settled, I realized I'd made an enormous commitment. Panic quickly ensued. At first, I told no one in the hope that nothing significant would come of it. Mother had other ideas.

I found out through friends about a woman who channeled an entity named Saraswati, the Hindu goddess of art and knowledge. The primary work She was doing through Her channel, Kim, was to help others learn to channel. Kim was giving a workshop in Los Angeles and Mother made sure I was there.

Saraswati taught me that the nature of channeling was to serve through devotion. It wasn't a trick to be displayed at a party after a few beers. She showed us how to set up an altar with fresh flowers and objects that held special meaning. We were to dress with care and prepare the space with reverence.

Then She moved from teaching the group as a whole, to working with each participant individually. My heart raced at the thought that I might have to go first. I tried to make myself small by hunching my body over and hiding behind the woman in front of me. It worked. With relief, I settled in to watch. Saraswati sat on the floor in front of the person She was working with, and held his hand as She spoke softly with a kind and gentle voice. Her entire demeanor said, *Take your time. Only do what feels comfortable.*

As the day wore on, I thought to myself, *I can do this.* She didn't work with me that day, nor the next morning. Up to that point, the only person at the workshop who knew about my agreement with Mother was my best friend, and I had asked her not to say anything to anyone. On the second day as we broke for lunch, Kim told me I would be first up for the afternoon session. After lunch, she pulled me over to the couch and told me to sit. I was confused because that was where Saraswati had been sitting to teach. When Kim tried to clip the microphone to my shirt, my stomach flipped over as if I'd just plunged down a giant rollercoaster hill.

"Wait a minute, what are you doing?" I asked her.

"Oh, we have to do it differently with you," Kim answered, "because Mother Mary and Saraswati are too big to both be in the room at the same time." My armpits broke out in a heavy sweat and I thought I might throw up.

"So," she continued, "Saraswati is going to come to my body and tell you what to do, and then She will leave so Mother Mary can come to your body."

I was too stunned to come up with a coherent, let alone cohesive, argument against this madness. What was she talking about? Then Kim was gone and Saraswati stood before me like a lioness, powerful and in command of everyone in the room. Where was the sweet hand-holder from only an hour before? She now was the Divine Goddess, and I trembled before Her.

Then, Saraswati pounced. *"Now, Beloved, repeat after*

me the prayer of union I give. I pray my heart to your heart, my love to your love, we are one heart, we are one love. My power to your power, we are one power. My wisdom to your wisdom, we are one wisdom. My truth to your truth, we are one truth. My vision to your vision, we are one vision."

As I repeated the prayer, my body began to fill with energy. It was as if someone had opened the top of my head and poured swirling weight into me. Every line I spoke expanded my body until I felt as though I took up all the space on the couch.

"Now, open yourself, Danielle!" Saraswati practically shouted, as She moved energy around the room with Her hands, *"Fly, run, crawl to your Divine Mother Mary and be one with Her!"* I felt Mother in the room before me, and like a child seeing her mother after a long separation, I flung myself at Her and spoke the final words of the prayer, *"I surrender my body to you now and always, so be it,"* and with that, Mother swallowed me whole. I felt Her rise up inside me and gently move me from the front of my body, to the back. It reminded me of the time I visited the Statue of Liberty and I stood gazing out from the little windows in the crown from the back of the crowded room. Those windows were my eyes, and Mother was in front of me staring out of them while I looked out from behind Her, deep within myself. It was bizarre, like an acid trip I hadn't chosen to take. It was frightening and I felt out of control. My body now seemed enormous because I could no longer feel where it ended. The only sensation of feeling I had was in my eyeballs. They burned with intensity.

Saraswati promptly left Kim's body. I panicked. Some people in the room gasped and began to cry. I started fighting the hold Mother had on my body. Saraswati had to come back. My senses were heightened and I could feel the force of Saraswati, like a controlled hurricane, as She entered the room and Kim's body. With both aspects of Divine Mother in body, in a tiny apartment, it felt like the roof would blow off of the building at any moment. Some people had to lie down because the energy became so overwhelming.

Saraswati calmed me down and soothed my fears by reminding me how extraordinary it felt to be one with Mother. And it did. It was just odd and new; not bad or painful. It felt like Mother breathed my body deeply like the bellows in a forge, instead of whatever automatic force that normally caused me to breath. Still today, She uses our breath to stay rooted in my body and to move Shakti or energy. I can't breathe as deeply as She can when She is in my body. She opened my eyes and everything was blurry, as if I were seeing without my glasses; but, I didn't even wear glasses.

More gasps and a few people started crawling on their knees to get to Her, and by default, me! I went beyond panic and into freak out. I was frightened by their naked need. A few had desperation in their eyes and it matched what I knew was inside me. Seeing through Mother's eyes stripped us all bare. I didn't want that kind of spirituality—I wanted intellectual spirituality—the kind you talked about but never had to reveal yourself with, the kind without intimacy. I absolutely did not want to be the purveyor of their salvation.

Again, Saraswati calmed me down, and told me that these people had been waiting their whole lives to be with Mother Mary in the body. That sobered me and pulled me back from my self-absorption. It was in that moment that my service began in earnest. Who was I to deny them their chance to commune with Mother? I would figure out the rest later. One by one, each person came forward to receive Her blessing. She spoke to a few and Her voice, as it came out of me, sounded like someone using their vocal cords for the first time. It was deep in timber but with a mix of gravel and breathiness. She touched everyone on the head or face while looking into their eyes. My arms and hands felt like they were numb; as if they had fallen asleep and didn't belong to me, but were moving just the same. The depth of love I saw shining from everyone's eyes as they gazed into Mother's eyes, was humbling to behold. Here was a kind of love I had never experienced before outside of my own heart. It was an outpouring of devotion that was unabashed in its beauty. It felt as if days were passing, but it turned out to be closer to thirty minutes from start to finish.

After Mother finished blessing each person, She left my body and I collapsed. I could barely walk. I spent the rest of the day prone and still. I was left with a profound sense of rightness about the whole thing. She kept me wrapped up in Her grace like a soft blanket made of light. Everyone was generous with their gratitude and encouragement that I continue to channel.

My roommate had to practically carry me onto the plane, and once we landed in Phoenix, he had to drive us home to Sedona. I spent two days in bed recovering. It was never that debilitating again. From that day on, whenever I channeled I was able to hold a little more of Mother's energy in my body. I'm still increasing the amount. When I let go of my inner clutter, I make room for Her presence.

Like my first commitment to recovery from food addiction, I needed a big experience to get my attention. If I'm to commit, I need a billboard with flashing lights and an obvious message. It was only after I made the commitment to channel Mother, and after Her display of power, that I became open to subtlety. I'm grateful that Mother and all my Spirit guides understand my needs better than I do. They know that if they want my attention, the message better be on something the size of an IMAX screen because as much as I want to embrace subtlety, it's very easy for me to ignore.

Mother Mary's commitment to me has shown me every day for the past twenty years the value of sticking with what works. I'm faced with a thousand distractions a day—and God knows I love a good distraction. Mother defines commitment like this—*"It means you are internally dedicated to your own happiness, peace of mind, and your own willingness to let go of suffering."* I still get hung up on that last bit, but I know what She means. If I want to thrive, I have to take actions to:

- Keep it simple
- Trust myself
- Let my heart be willing
- Forgive the past
- Remember I am one with all of life
- Embrace my spiritual life
- Love my shadow
- Allow miracles
- Do something I love everyday
- Stay committed to my whole Self

These simple actions keep me in the flow of the river that empties into the wide ocean of faith, where I am held and cherished. Being held in faith allows me to feel I can face anything that life brings to me. That feeling inspires me to show up for all the commitments in my life, which form the building blocks of my spiritual and emotional foundation.

CHAPTER 23
Faith

Faith and love intertwine like the roots of a tree, solid and able to sustain life. This last teaching in the collection provides insight and guidance concerning the foundation of love that you and I are building, and which will carry you the farthest. Faith is something that most people have struggled with at different times in their lives. It's hard to believe in something if you're not exactly sure what it is, or how you feel about it.

Faith is a word in your culture that is used often. You begin hearing it from a very young age. Sometimes it's in relation to religion. Other times, it's in relation to just everyday living. You are told to have faith, but rarely are you informed as to how to create faith, or even what it really is.

Faith is the experience of Oneness.
It's the feeling of connection you have to all
of life.

Faith is something that's created slowly over time; it never happens instantly. Belief can happen instantly, but faith does not. There's a great difference between belief and faith. Belief is something that you don't have quite as much invested in. Beliefs can come and go. They change as you change. What you believe now is not necessarily what you believed ten years ago, five years ago, or even one year ago.

Beliefs are built on concepts. If someone explains something to you, like I'm doing now, what may happen is that you have a new belief about faith. Then you have to take that belief out into the rainy night, and do something with it; or not. A belief is something that you *hear* as truth. You may have heard it before a thousand times, but suddenly it strikes a chord of truth in you, and so you say, *Yes now I understand.* Or maybe you're hearing something for the first time and you think that, *Yes, I believe that.* You're not sure why, but you believe it. Now will come the process of going out into the world and turning your belief into faith, so that you can feel more connected to your own life and the life around you.

A belief is the beginning of an idea or concept, and as you go out into the world with that belief, synchronicity starts to occur. All of a sudden, everyone's talking about it. You're reading about it in magazines. You hear something about it on television. Someone you haven't spoken to in years lets you know that they just heard the same thing, not a month ago! Whereas before it was nowhere, now it's everywhere. Each time this comes to you, something is added to the belief and a different facet is introduced. Your belief settles in a little more. Sometimes a new side of the same belief comes up and you think, *No, that doesn't resonate with me.* This is the process of coming to faith that happens once a belief takes root inside of you.

For everyone, the process of coming to faith will happen in its own time, not necessarily in yours. In order for you to create the energy of faith, the belief has to be proven to you. No matter how strong your faith is in some areas, or no matter how deeply you believe something, very few humans are willing to bet the farm on it if they don't get some kind of *proof.* It's hard to formulate a belief into faith, if synchronicity doesn't happen.

Synchronicity is how you go out and prove that belief. If you read something here and go out into the world and there's no synchronicity, then it's not time for you to build faith around that truth. It's a seed that's been planted and will grow at another time. But when you go out and all of a sudden you're seeing this new belief in action everywhere, hearing about it everywhere, or you can't stop thinking about it and want to explore it more deeply for yourself, then you know that you're working towards building faith around this something that has come to you.

Faith is not black or white. Faith is something that is added to each day, every day that you're alive in your body. I feel that you're often a little hard on yourself, particularly around faith. People will tell you to just relax and have a little faith. How can you be a spiritual person and not have faith? The answer is—*easily*—because you're a person that is continually changing and growing. It's not one or the other.

> Faith is a state of being that is constantly evolving for each of you. You build its strength when you're on a path of consciously discovering what your beliefs mean to you. You mustn't just take what someone else believes and making it your own verbatim. You take what you study, what you hear and absorb, and what comes to you in your life, and you ingest it. You sit with it and discover for yourself what feels believable and right for you. This is how you build faith.

You cannot build faith if you don't trust your own beliefs. Don't simply take on what sounds good, or what others think sounds good to them. You must take the time to examine your own beliefs and sit with how *you* feel about things; only *then* will it translate into faith. You can act faithfully, you can appear faithful, you can even behave in a faithful way—but it's doubtful you will reap the benefits of faith, and the primary benefit is peace.

When you are in the state of faith, you are
at peace.

Faith is something that can be passed from one person to another. It's a very powerful energy. Let's say I tell you to go see a certain person for something and you have faith in me but not in them. You decide to go to see them anyway, because what I told you struck a chord of truth in you. You may not be sure why, but you know you need to go, and you have faith in me. That's belief. I made a recommendation. It struck a chord of truth in you so you sat with it. You felt it. Then you took action by going, and what happened was wonderful for you. You grew, learned, blossomed, and healed. You began to have faith in what that person is doing.

So, you pass that along to the next person, the next, and the next. All of a sudden, once you start trusting yourself and following your beliefs to the best of your ability, you generate the energy of faith. There's a strength and power in that energy, which creates a deeper connection to the Divine and to Self. This is at the heart, or root, of all faith; that there's a connection between each of you—there is Oneness.

This is what faith is; it's connection.
Connection to the Divine, connection to
yourself, and connection to each other.

The only way you can build faith is by trusting your beliefs and building on them; one step at a time—one person at a time—one experience at a time. Ultimately, what I want is for you to have faith in yourself. Having faith in things outside of yourself is important, but having faith in *you* is equally important. When you have faith in yourself, recognize your own connection to the Divine, and then feel the connectedness, you don't just take what other people say as fact without examining it. You don't have blind faith in the world around you.

For so long, human beings have allowed others to dictate their beliefs and the structure of their faith. There have always been people who said no to this paradigm and gone their own way. More and more of you are like this now, but some are still saying that it may be fine for others but not for them. You honor the beliefs of others, but don't choose to follow them yourself. Sometimes it seems easier to just be told what to believe, what to look like, and how you to behave. That's all right to pay attention to as far as getting along in your society, because there are certain laws that you're asked to abide by, whether you agree with them or not. Making the decision as to whether or not to abide by them is an individual choice. Sometimes it makes your life easier to do so. Sometimes it does not.

At the heart of it, you're each on a path to discovery of Self, and it will never be easy to have blind faith in what others tell you that you should have blind faith in. You can watch others use that belief to great results and happiness, but I'm sorry to say you are not amongst that group. What you're being asked to do in your own life is to become yourself. You are an individual, but not separate. As an individual, you must discover your own set of beliefs, and then allow them to change as you change, never getting too attached. When one comes and you feel the truth in it, let it be for today. Let it be in that moment.

*In an ultimate sense, faith has little to do
with beliefs themselves, or their specifics.
The particulars of your beliefs simply serve
as a structure in which to support your
enlightenment or Oneness. Once that
enlightenment occurs, the faith is constant,
and the belief in things falls away and
becomes unnecessary. For now, your beliefs
are very important. Allow them to be fluid
and open. Allow them to shift and change.
And please, please don't apologize when
they do.*

Just as you don't require others to justify their beliefs, you don't have to justify your own. Part of owning Self, or owning your beliefs, is just that; letting them be your own. You know that they may or may not be shared by others, and that's all right. They're building their own faith and it won't look exactly like yours. Faith is something that comes to you at all times—whether your world is quiet or in chaos—faith is there. Try not to believe that you have to be in a certain place in order to build your faith. Just invite it in. Know that it's there for you, every day that you live. You are growing in your faith whether you now it or not. You don't have to force it.

*I'd like for you to very strongly consider
accepting the part of yourself that needs
God or the Divine to prove itself to you in
order for you to build stronger faith. Accept
the part of you that is human and needs*

reassurance, synchronicity, and validation. Welcome that into your life, into your world. Call it to you.

If something is introduced to you— *anything*—and you feel a chord of truth is struck inside of you, don't be afraid to ask the universe for help; *I feel the truth. If you want me to do anything with it, show me. Oh, and make it obvious!*

Ask for what you need from the Divine. Don't be afraid. Don't believe, if you can possibly help it, that you should be anywhere that you're not. You are where you are. Some days you will be able to touch your faith more deeply than others.

Keep asking. Recognize that there's a pattern to how your faith is built. Become familiar with that pattern and become a part of it. Actively participate.

If something you're reading now strikes a chord, then let your prayer for the week be to *show* me. Show me what this is for me. Make it obvious. I want to know. I want to go more deeply into my life, this world, and the Divine. The more active you are in wanting and requesting to be a part of this, the easier it is to show you and take you by the hand and say, *here it is!*

There are many different ways to experience faith. Most importantly for human beings, faith tends to happen when good things come your way; when things either turn out the way you wanted or anticipated them to. Then a camaraderie with God tends to happen. There's a lot of backslapping and everyone's very excited, thinking, *Look! We did it!*

But when things *don't* go so well or tragedy strikes, you'll often hear people say that they had great faith all their lives until *this* happened; how could God let this happen? They're faith disappears. People also like to say that their faith is being tested. As your education system is discovering, tests don't really work very well, so we generally don't employ them. We find that the anxiety they produce far outweighs the benefit. What life *does* present are opportunities. You and only you can know if your faith is conditional. This is something you have to discover.

> Take some time over the next two weeks during your active meditations and just explore what your faith feels like to you. When is it strongest? When is it either at its weakest or nonexistent? Start to notice if your faith is conditional. Remember my words, that ultimately, faith is based on your connection to the Divine; not what happens in your life. Faith is based on your connection to the Divine. And when I say Divine, I mean *creation* or *life—not* a particular entity or deity.

Your life is only one among many. It won't always go the way you want it to go. Yes, there are things that happen in this world that are tragic, horrible—even inconceivable— and often to innocent people and children. What you have to understand is that each of you has lived lifetimes upon lifetimes. There's an intertwining of karma that stretches over thousands of years. Many Souls are bound together in ways that you cannot understand. You are not God in total. You are an aspect of God, but you are not God the One. Your finite vision must always be taken into consideration when you're trying to explore the question of faith. You will never have all the answers. Even now, you won't get the answers to some of your greatest questions because it's in the questioning that you grow. For *some* things you may get a satisfactory answer, but don't allow your faith to be based on that. All of that will fall away. You're only human for a short time, though some of you longer than others.

> Don't allow your faith to be based on
> something that can be broken. If you do,
> then it's not really faith that you have, but
> a belief that has not matured into faith yet.
> Faith is something that doesn't change the
> way beliefs do. It only grows. Faith is the
> solid knowing that you are connected to the
> Divine, that you are the Divine, that we are
> all One, and for some strange, inexplicable
> reason, everything is going to be okay. That
> is faith. When your house is demolished
> after a tornado, when you've just lost a
> loved one, when you're in debt and have no
> job but for some strange reason you know,
> you absolutely know, that it's going to be
> okay, that's faith. It won't ever change
> unless you choose to cut yourself off from
> it.

The energy of faith was designed not to change, so that

you could always recognize it. It's that faith, that knowing that you will be all right, that gives you the courage to know yourself; to begin to explore your own beliefs, to experiment with things, to go here, to go there, to try this, to try that. For you to feel safe, faith must stay the same. It must be the solid center that no matter where you move is always there. It must be the one thing that you can count on every, single day. If faith were to change too much in its feeling, it would be too easy to lose; *Wait, where did my faith go?* You have enough of that in your life. Enlightenment is not an easy path—simple, yes—easy, *no*.

There had to be one thing in your existence, lifetime after lifetime after lifetime, that for each and every person was the same, as that's what brings you all together in the end. Christian, Buddhist, Extremist, Atheist—it doesn't matter because ultimately, it's there for everyone and doesn't necessarily have to go with a sense of spirituality. It's God's promise to humanity; it's your assurance that there's something within you that knows the truth, is there for you, and will see you through everything. Without faith, you could not have survived.

Faith is an energy that binds you together in a wonderful way. It brings common ground where it seems there is none. Faith is the one thing that triumphs over all fear, all pain, and all death. It's the feeling of being okay that's in your memory before you came to a human body, your memory of being One with all, of being a part of source energy—the All That Is, before you left and chose to have a Soul inhabiting a physical body. That memory carries you from lifetime to lifetime. It sustains you. It is the energy that carries you back. You don't have to place your faith in a particular belief, but it's the exploration of your beliefs that bring you to your faith. Once you find that within yourself, you can't really explain it. Your life could be falling apart all around you, but you feel okay.

For those of you who have been coming to me for a little while, I want you to recognize that there are different levels of faith. You can focus on this as little or as much as you like. If you're reading this right now with your heart as well as your mind, you will recognize that at the core of all my teachings is the energy to help you find your faith through consciousness. This is why I come to this body.

You can have a little faith or a lot of faith. My preference would be a lot of faith. What you'll find if you focus on faith is that your life becomes easier. What falls away is your belief, or misplaced faith, in things that your culture and society tell you that you should have faith in. For a long time you've probably been told if you own certain things, look a certain way, and have certain amounts of money, your faith will give you a wonderful life; the life you've always dreamed of. Then... it doesn't happen. What I'm asking you to consider is a life that's *based* on faith, rather than only looking for faith when you think you need it or when you're feeling a bit empty.

Instead of using it as a tool, let faith be everything to you. Put your faith first, before anything else. What exactly does that mean? If at the heart of things you know that everything's always going to be okay, there's not too much to worry about. If you're placing faith in your connection to the Divine, what that means is that you're seeking to quiet the mind.

> Give to me the mind that's programmed to
> be in control, to organize, to try and figure
> it all out; give that all to me. When you do,
> you'll begin to care less and less about the
> objects outside of you. Once this happens,
> they will no longer hold or possess you.

You'll care from a standpoint of compassion, but not from possession. Letting go of your possessions doesn't necessarily mean that you're *physically* giving them all away; you're not going to just hang on to a pair of sandals and a robe. It means that you surrender the *hold* they have on you. When you're focused on your faith, when you awaken in the morning going on the premise that everything today is going to be okay, it means that you are utterly and completely connected. It's not just you walking through your day, but all of existence walking with you! What could you possibly be lacking? What could you possibly need to worry about, when everything that you need is right here with you, in every moment?

Faith is about having a *knowing*. When you focus on faith, the doubts are quiet until they begin to fall away all together. If you focus on the doubt, if you give it credence, if you give it too much of a voice, then you're making your choice, and it's doubt that will go through your day with you rather than faith. Knowing that everything is going to be okay means that if you're to be in Atlanta, all signs will point to Atlanta. If you need to be in Africa working on humanitarian aid, then someone will hand you a ticket.

Simplify your life as you go about it. Often, faith is particularly difficult for spiritual people who also enjoy great intelligence and humor. Many of you like to look at the world with irony, and you think *other* people are crazy. You may poke fun at them, thinking it's great to laugh and have humor about your world, your life, and your own journey, but be careful that your intellectual Self doesn't stand between you and your faith.

Something else I'd ask you to look at when
you examine your faith is how you feel
about faith intellectually. Is there a voice, a

lovely intellectual voice inside, that whispers to you, *"People of faith speak in tongues, roll in the aisle, and handle snakes. Why are people who profess to have faith blowing themselves up? Who are these people? Am I one of those people?"* What do you *really* believe; not just the part of you that you'd love to have be gorgeously spiritual and walking on water, but *all* of you—what do you believe about faith? If you discover that parts of yourself are afraid of faith or want to demean it as silly, don't reject those parts. Love them. Forgive them. Surrender them. At some point, you must accept that you're a person of faith, and that to live any other way doesn't bring you happiness. Just because you're a person of faith and choose to live in that faith, to focus on that faith every day, does not make you even the tiniest bit less intelligent. It doesn't make you ridiculous in any way. It simply gives you the freedom that you're seeking.

I'll give you a little exercise to help you begin to focus on faith. Some of my exercises can appear a bit simplistic in the beginning, but stick with them and you'll find things starting to happen for you.

From the moment you awaken in the morning, start to turn everything over to me—your shower, your breakfast, your

commute, your work, your telephone calls—
everything. Anything you do, just before
you do it, take a little breath and say, *"This
belongs to you, Mother, this belongs to you."*

That, ultimately, is the practice of faith. You're not abdicating your life, you're not turning over all your responsibilities to me in the respect that now you'll have none. What you are doing is making the conscious choice, in each moment, to say that you choose the Divine rather than the mind that is fretting, that wants to control and is constantly worried about avoiding pain; the mind that is ten steps ahead, or ten years ahead, or ten years behind. The mind is the part of Self that fills you with doubt.

With each thing you turn over, keep saying
to yourself throughout the day, *"If there's
anything you want me to know, just make it
obvious. Show me. Show me. Show me."*

Focus on the knowing inside of you, that everything is going to be okay. This puts you in the space of listening to the Divine. When your mind is not completely taken up with doubts, fantasies, the future, and the past, then all of a sudden there's room for you. There's room for me. There's room for us to commune together. When that happens, things start to unfold effortlessly.

When you are afraid, say, *"This belongs to
you, Mother."* Anything that comes up for
you during the day that you start to get
lost in through past or future thinking of
Self and others, say, *"This belongs to you,*

Mother. I am here, I am now, I am present."
You will probably chuckle a few times the
first few times you reach for a glass of
water and say, *"I give it to you, Mother."*
But this is the practice that will get you
focused on what you really need in this life.

None of you are here to be tourists this time. You're not here to observe and you're certainly not here to stay in denial. You're here to live your life as you *are*—not how you wish you *could* be, or how you might *pretend* to be, but how you are *now*. Will it change? Yes, but to be present with yourself *now* is where the power is, always. Nothing is more powerful than you, as you are right now.

Being present and focused on your faith means no one can take it from you unless you let them. No one can talk you out of your faith unless you let them. No matter what jail they put you in, no matter what they do to your body or mind, they cannot take your faith. They cannot. Faith is constant and never changing. It's always there. It's always growing in power. Let faith be the belief that you explore over the next few weeks. See where it takes you. My guess is that it will take you to faith.

MEDITATION:

Sit quietly and close your eyes. As you breathe deeply, I'd like for you to imagine that you're breathing in through the top of your head and breathing out through the bottoms of your feet. With each breath, you feel more and more a part of the earth, a part of the chair that you're sitting in, a part of the people around you, a part of all that's in the room.

Consciously connect yourself with all that you feel. Now find the place within you where your faith dwells. The knowing that no matter what, you will be all right; you will be okay.

As the breath, the energy, passes through your whole body, from the top of the head to the bottom of the feet, focus on your faith. Now close the crown chakra and just breathe normally. If you so choose, commit to yourself now that you will trust in the synchronicities that come to you; that you will believe the validation that comes to you. Commit to being present, and explore your beliefs so that they will strengthen the faith that already exists within you. Commit to finding the awe in synchronicity, and that you will allow yourself to feel the gratitude that comes with validation.

Most importantly, commit to focus on your faith. Even if old beliefs tell you to do otherwise, you will choose the new beliefs that are being constantly validated all around you. In this you will place your trust. It's my greatest desire for each and every one of you, that for as long as you draw breathe into your body, you will know, no matter what's going on in your life, that you're all right and that everything's going to be okay. This is a mother's desire for her children.

Breathe that in. Now place your hands together in the Mudra of prayer, over your heart chakra. Let your chin drop just a little bit. Take a deep breath and say within yourself, "*I have faith.*"

Now take three deep breaths and on exhalation let go of the meditation.

Wonderful. You are all brilliant in your faith, in your beauty, in your expression of Self. I thank you for allowing me to serve you.

Namaste ~

CHAPTER 24
Crisis of faith

"Danielle, wake up! Your car is on fire!" my roommate shouted.

I bolted up in bed like a marionette whose strings had been yanked. Adrenalin pumped through my body. I was filled with instant energy. I looked at the clock—1:30 am. I jumped out of bed and shouted back to my roommate, *"I'll call 911!"*

My outward demeanor was dead calm with laser focus. I threw on a pair of sweatpants and a sweatshirt because I felt too vulnerable to deal with the situation naked. I picked up the phone, called emergency services, and told the woman on the other end where I lived and that my car was on fire in my driveway. I know in my bones I gave the correct address, but that didn't prevent the fire truck from ending up somewhere else.

My three roommates and I gathered our two dogs and one cat and headed to the front door. We opened it with caution. We were greeted by the sight of my car engulfed in twenty-foot high flames. We froze in the doorway, rooted in shock. It felt surreal, as if we were part of a tour on a movie set. The bonfire that was formerly my car raged out of control to the left of us. On the right was a majestic old oak tree whose branches draped over the roof of the house. Our escape route to the street was straight ahead through the front lawn. My body was numb with fear and my thoughts raced. If I left the safety of the front doorway, would the flames reach out and grab me? What if my car exploded and we were ripped apart by burning metal and were burned to ash? I was paralyzed. A moment later those thoughts drained out of me like water through a sieve and there was only empty silence left. As if we were suddenly released by an unseen hand, all at once, we made a quick dash to the street, all two and four legged beings accounted for.

On the street, I noticed that one of my roommates' car was smoking, the interior a blackened ruin. By the look of it, someone had tried but failed to burn hers. The street was packed on both sides with parked cars, but we were the only ones targeted. A new fear awakened inside me. I looked around. Our neighbors stood gawking at us from their lawns. Not one person came over to ask if we were okay, or if everyone was out of the house. As we listened to the sound of the siren moving farther away and then stopping, not one person moved to call 911 again.

This was like no fire I had ever read about. Where were the people rushing to help? Where was the person who volunteered to run back into the house if that's what was called for? *"What the hell!"* my mind screamed. I felt an old rage burn inside of me. These people couldn't even be bothered to muster up the same level of interest you would give any stranger on the street. I was choking on their apathy. I felt forgotten and dismissed. My stomach heaved and I almost threw up. My body flashed hot then cold. I was going into shock. *"Please call 911 again!"* I shouted at them. With reluctance, one neighbor finally turned and headed inside. After an agonizing few minutes, we heard from a distance the faint sound of the fire truck's siren starting up again. Time seemed to stretch out and slow down, making it seem as though it took hours for the fire truck to finally reach us.

In those precious minutes of waiting for the firemen to arrive, the fire leapt even higher into the thirty-year-old oak tree on the other side of the house. The heavy branches that hung over the roof burst into flames, catching the roof on fire moments later. I loved that tree. It was gnarled and heavy with age and experience. I felt it was a guardian of our home, watching over us and protecting us from harm. But it couldn't withstand the darkness that humans wield with devastating effect. I stood helplessly by, watching the tree, my car, and my home being taken from me by circumstances beyond my control. We were renting the house from a kind man who had built most of the house himself. He told me it had been a labor of love. I cursed everyone and everything for destroying it.

At one o'clock in the morning, four years after I had begun my journey with Mother Mary, I was homeless, without a car, and with no way to even call my boyfriend for help, as this was long before the widespread use of cell phones. The firefighters finally arrived and began working to put out the fire.

A woman from the Red Cross showed up and sat down with us on the curb across from our front yard. She was a petite woman with average looks and a plump body. Given her attitude, she seemed about as happy to be there as we were. She asked us if we had a place to go, because the firefighters had deemed the smoke damage to intense to allow us to remain in the house. We did, but had no way to make the necessary calls. A young woman from across the street finally approached and offered to let us use her phone. Once we were in her house, she informed us that the neighbors did not like what went on in our house, and told us she'd heard grumblings of devil worship. Fear slid down my spine for a second time that night in relation to our neighbors. *What?!* Were we not living in a good neighborhood, in Seattle, in the year 1998?

From a hidden place deep inside me, I blamed Mother for allowing something this dark to slither into our work. I didn't sign up to be burned at the stake. It was in that moment that my crisis of faith began. I felt as if the rug had been pulled out from under me, again. Had God lost my file, or worse, put it in the punishment pile? Insidious doubt began to creep in. Since blame and self-pity are my go to feelings, it became a perfect storm that lasted a few years. It's amazing to me that I never once thought about turning away from Mother. That was Her grace, not mine.

The fire burned away my veneer and exposed my inherent mistrust of Mother and life in general. I slowly stopped doing all the things that had brought me closer to Her, like writing in my journal, meditating, and sharing my confused feelings with friends. I reached out less and less for support with my food addiction, and as a result the old feeling of depression began to take hold of my mind and heart again. The world's colors dulled and lost their luster and I was left feeling numb.

The result of my blame and self-pity was rebellion. So began a four-year tug-of-war between Mother and myself. She would give me clear, personal directions, I would say, "*No.*" The initial high of imagining myself in control would commence, followed by the train wreck of events my trying to control things brought about.

Every time I seized control and things fell apart, my old paradigm of faith cracked. The hammer that finally shattered my old belief in faith was the dissolution of my first marriage while I was pregnant with my son. If I wanted to live a life of love and devotion, it had to be founded on a faith that would stand, no matter what. It needed to be as consistent as the sunrise and as easy to access as my breath. But it must also be roomy like Alaska, so I could still punch and kick when I needed to.

I'm convinced that I surrendered more during my pregnancy than at any other time in my life. Mother gathered the pieces of me, and like the place where a bone knits together after a break, I felt stronger than I ever had in my life. The spirit of my son as he grew inside me, Mother, and a small army of friends gave endless support.

I sat at my altar every morning and poured my thoughts and feelings onto paper. I prayed aloud for the strength to accept myself and do what needed to be done each day. I meditated so I could be still and feel Mother. I meditated so I could feel myself. I called a friend every day. I showed up and I served others.

What finally emerged from the ashes of that long ago fire were five words; **It will be all right**. I had not known that since I was a small child. It was not something I told myself or tried to convince myself of—I *felt* it. Being okay became experiential.

Before the night of the fire, my constant prayer had been, *"Thy will, not mine, be done."* The night of the fire, I walked into God's flame and burned for four years. It purged from me the "fantasy" faith, where only good things happen to me because I'm a good person; the faith within which violence doesn't exist, and sticky sweet love saves the day.

Mother asked me to give up everything for Her and be naked on my knees at Her feet. She sings inside of me Her grace and forgiveness. She releases me from the bondage of fear like a ball of yarn that's released to unravel its glorious color across the floor.

In the midst of the pain I had caused myself, my husband, and our families, as I held my son for the first time, I knew there were no mistakes. This became the cornerstone of my faith. I saw myself as human. We are given the gift of life and the gift of choice. Sometimes our choices lead to pain and other times to joy. We can only do the best we can with what is inside—not what I want or believe *should* be inside, but what *is* inside.

Emerging from the fire, glowing with my sense of being *all right* with *what is*, created a faith that is solid today because of my difficulties *and* achievements, laughter *and* pain, all of which is normal and not something I have to fix about myself or run away from.

It is simply my beautiful life.

Thank you for reading our book!
Beloved Publications is dedicated to sharing
Mother Mary's grace with all who wish to receive
it. You can find more of Her teachings
at www.belovedpublications.com. If you enjoyed
this book and would like to support Mother's
teachings, please share it with a loved one through
social media or at your kitchen table. You can
leave a review on amazon.com, goodreads.com, or
anywhere else you're moved to.
We are grateful for your generosity of spirit.

ACKNOWLEDGEMENTS

I wish to give giant hugs and kisses to Deborah Streit-George, Madisyn Taylor, Camille Stranger, Robbie Holz, Linda Gooding, and Robin Mastro for their unconditional support, honesty, and love. You all gave me exactly what I needed to bring this book to life. Thank you, Janice Corrales and Sara Boyd, for your service that started it all. Deborah Streit George and Jo Spring, you made our words shine; thank you. A big thank you to my son Ivan, for his smile and the best belly laugh ever. I love you. To the Beloved Publications community, I am grateful for all these years of support and love. I couldn't have done any of this without you. And of course to my Divine Mother Mary who holds my hand no matter what and never lets me fall. I love you and thank you from my bones for this book and all you have brought to my life. I am yours always.

31878475R00182

Made in the USA
Middletown, DE
15 May 2016